Penybont Llanerch Emrys

WALKS

Peter Keen

Published by Peter Keen
Publishing Partner: Paragon Publishing, Rothersthorpe
First published 2022

ISBN 978-1-78222-958-2

Book design, layout and production management by Into Print
www.intoprint.net
+44 (0)1604 832149

Penybont Bridge

Acknowledgements

Many thanks to Nick and Heather Rees for proof reading this little book.

I am grateful to many local people for sharing their knowledge of routes and history of the area, especially Graham Forester and Billy Morgan for their lifelong knowledge of the area.

Contents

Introduction

The earth is a small place and yet, we will never see it all in our lifetime. We have to restrict our viewing to places that interest us and that are accessible within our means. Travel to distant places has become much more possible to the average person than ever before. There are still people who have never left their home location throughout their life. Others travel widely by the different methods available. We all have different viewpoints on these matters, to which we are entitled. Years ago, travel was not possible for ordinary folk. They would work in the factory or down the mine or on the farm for six days per week. The time, funds and means to travel were unavailable to most people until recent years.

Penybont Llanerch Emrys is situated a few yards inside Wales. There are several Penybonts and to distinguish our own Penybont, we may give it the full title. To avoid typing, we shall simply call it Penybont from now on. The name derives from "Peny" meaning "head of" and "bont" meaning bridge. Thomas Penson lived from 1790 to 1859 and he was the local county surveyor who was charged with the task of building bridges to allow access through the area. Penybont bridge was one of his jobs.

There has only been one real drought on record in Britain when it didn't rain for eight weeks. That was in 1976. Some people brought out a new theory called global warming and they said the summer of 1976 would from then on be the shape of things to come. From that time forward we would be dry roasted and everything would turn brown. As I said, we are all entitled to our opinion. The only thing is that opinions tend to get proved or disproved by the events that follow their ventilation. What we can say is that the summer of 1976 has never yet been repeated - although this year, 2022, is threatening to be one of extremes and previous records may yet be broken. Wales is a land of hills and valleys. Long before roads, it rained and the rain ran down the hills and into the rivers which run through every valley. Later on, people came to live here and wanted to get about. They needed bridges to cross rivers. Hence, Penybont. I don't know the date of constructing Penybont bridge but, it is marked on the 1841 local tithe map so it may have been one of Penson's earlier works. "Llanerch" means glade or clearing and "Emrys" is a boy's name. Whoever Emrys of Penybont was, we don't know. What we can surmise is that when most of the area was tree covered, old Emrys had a clearing upon which the village was constructed. It was near enough to the river to have an easily gained water supply but, just far enough away to avoid the annual flooding. Hence we can comment that Emrys was in planning terms, a man of intelligence, in contrast to some current planning officials who build in flood plains.

If travel was still impossible, the Penybont area would, to me, be a desirable place to live. Here is a land of hills and valleys; a scenic delight. The handiwork of God our great Creator is shown in all this beauty. We all have different views as to what constitutes a desirable place. Many people express the desire to live in the countryside but, having invested in such a place, remark that there is nothing to do. They travel somewhere else rather than remaining at home. Some desire the "madding crowd", the entertainments, the shopping malls, the parks, the manicured settings. The desire of many to live in the countryside is not carefully researched and yet, millions are making the move out of town. They say that they like the smell of the fresh air. Fresh air has no smell at all. If you can smell the air, that odour is due to a pollutant. In the countryside, this is probably the rich aroma of animal slurry that is sprinkled liberally on the fields in a process known as "muck spreading". There will also incidentally be a lot of this sticky substance all over the roads and the sides and wheel arches of your car. Some of the local farmers are adept at laying muck on the roads and bringing their fields out onto the highway. I knew one farmer who got away with this for years because the council would not tackle him on it. Suffice it to say that there are farmers who run clean and pleasant establishments while others are grubby urchins who regularly foul the local roads and don't bother cleaning up afterwards. The councils also soil the roads nearly every night from October to April. Hundreds of tons of salt, grit, mud and other substances added to the mix, are strewn thickly. Salt is deliquescent and absorbs water from the atmosphere to produce a slimy soup that is dangerous and highly corrosive to the road structure and your car. Another common countryside smell is smoke. This is not from stubble burning that was outlawed some years ago but from building developers cutting down trees and hedges and burning them to make way for housing. They call it slash and burn in the Amazon. It goes on in our countryside too. Some express the desire for the peace and serenity of the countryside. That, too, is disappearing because of the rapid movement of the population out of town. Most villages are quickly expanding as thousands of acres of farmland are built on every year. The chances are that when you move out of town to your peaceful idyllic setting, you will, within a few short years, be in the middle of a building site. You can of course avoid this, by purchasing a property on the edge of a cliff. The unfortunate consequence of this is that the cliffs give way and your home descends in bits down to the beach below.

What we are saying is that there are pros and cons to living in the countryside. If your love of the countryside is genuine and you like countryside activities, Penybont is a good place to be. If you prefer entertainment and city life, think no further west than Oswestry that Shropshire Council is rapidly developing and enlarging. There you have twelve supermarkets in the vicinity and all the hubbub that you can put up with. If that's not enough concrete for you, the even more heavily developed areas of Shrewsbury and Telford are nearby. If however you like identifying plants, walking the lanes and hills, enjoying the good old country smells and you don't mind your car and your shoes always being a shade of brown, Penybont may be the place for you to roam.

This little book details a few local walks that I have enjoyed and, I hope you do too. Each walk can be completed in reverse. That is your choice. I have provided details and photographs for each walk in one direction but, if you prefer to do them in the opposite direction, that's just fine.

I can't emphasise too many times that the countryside is nearly all owned and though we can walk, we need to respect the countryside code which basically says that we should close all gates we open, cause no harm to plants and animals and leave no litter. We can enjoy nature without disturbing and spoiling it. We often think of the Amazon as a place where environmental damage is caused but, in Britain, thousands of acres of greenfield are concreted every year. This is deplorable and unsustainable and it is fair to say that most damage is development related and therefore attributable to land owners and planning authorities. Walkers are generally nature lovers who will look after the environment and are there to enjoy it.

Things to be aware of

If having read the introduction, you are still interested in coming to walk round Penybont; there are a few things you need to be aware of.

Regarding walks, there are many available. There are not many signed footpaths but, designated paths can be identified on Ordnance Survey maps. Many footpath signs have been removed. If you look carefully at the posts you will sometimes see four pins with a little remaining yellow fragment under each one. The main part of the footpath sign has been removed. You will also see footpath access prevented with hedging as shown in the example below.

Would you like to try this stile? It is an official footpath marked on the OS map

I have tried hard to describe public rights of way, and to distinguish between these and walks that should be cleared with local landowners before proceeding.

There are no public car parks in or around Penybont. There is a pull-in on the B4396 about half a mile east of the village but there are a few places where a car can be left without causing a problem. There is a public car park in Llangedwyn by the mill and accessed just off the B4396 on the lane to Bwlch-y-ddar. Don't park in gateways. Even if it appears obvious that they haven't been used in ages, access will be required as soon as you leave your vehicle. There is a bus service through the Tanat valley but there are only two or sometimes three runs per day. The service is the Tanat Bus service 79A and times are available online.

Penybont is on the corner between three Ordnance Survey Explorer Maps. If you bring three maps and try to spread them out on the ground there will be a strong wind and you will end up with a bad temper before you start. I arranged a custom map to be printed by Ordnance Survey with Penybont in its centre. That makes life much easier. An alternative method is to subscribe to Ordnance Survey and that allows you to download maps to your mobile phone. The unfortunate thing with this lovable technology is that a few inches of screen on your phone can't fit much map on it so you will spend hours scrolling and then lose where you are. We live in days when knowledge is increased but, knowledge and sense are different parameters that don't necessarily go together. Get yourself a map on a sheet of paper and a plastic cover for it and that's one recipe for unhappiness removed from your day. There is hardly any mobile phone signal in or around Penybont. You will find universal good signal strength in Cambodia but not in Britain. Mobile coverage for Britain is in private ownership and the companies will not provide coverage to rural areas. These companies only provide good coverage in major conurbations. They quote coverage in excess of 90% of Britain but, what they mean is that over 90% of the population has provision. There is a much lower percentage of the area of the country covered. Therefore, don't expect your phone to work round Penybont. Sometimes it will but, mostly the service is extremely patchy.

It has been known to rain in Penybont and for the rain to be continuous for several days on the run. On average there are about 170 rainy days each year in Powys which is about half of them. Sometimes, the weather is lovely. The general principle is that if you plan a walk some weeks ahead, there will be a mist or howling wind, or rain and often, there will be all three. It's best if you can avoid planning ahead and just respond to the call to the hills when the weather is hospitable. The main joy of a walk in this area is the scenic views. When they are shrouded in murk, they cannot be appreciated and you would have had a cheaper and more comfortable day in your arm chair reading this book and enjoying the photographs taken in more favourable conditions.

As I type these words, it's early April 2022 and so far has been rather cold. April of 2021 was the coldest since 1922. Despite the rapidly growing tide of opinion in favour of global warming, it is unlikely that you will be comfortable without several layers of warm clothing. Many years of motorcycle riding and walking has taught me that there is no such a thing as waterproof clothing and, if you do manage to get yourself utterly sealed, you will get wet from the inside. The best strategy is to avoid really inclement days and take a few layers in your rucksack just in case. Umbrellas are no good unless the weather happens to be really calm which, on the hills is unusual. You can of course buy a Davek which is designed to cope with weather but, it will set you back over £100 and you will end up leaving it somewhere if the rain stops. And, even a Davek is not much good when you negotiate a thorn bush.

The lanes round Penybont are fairly quiet apart from the B4396 which is very busy. However, the lanes are bendy and you need to be ready to dive for the hedge when a vehicle is coming. At dawn or dusk, you need light clothing, preferably something reflective. We live in a period when pedestrians and cyclists have precedence over vehicles in many situations. They've just brought out a new Highway Code to say so but, while it's nice to die in the right, it's even better to stay in one piece rather than having to be scraped up. Experience has shown that some vehicles have drivers who manage straight lines but not bends. On the road connecting Penybont to Llansantfraid, little piles of glass mark the spots where mirrors of passing vehicles were mounted at the same height. Little piles of coloured glass chippings show where light clusters were also involved. Just be aware that motor vehicles are driven but not always in a smart manner. If you want to see another day, you need to be one step ahead and ready to get up the bank.

OS maps are protected by copyright and I cannot therefore publish OS maps to show your walking routes. Instead, I have produced my own very simple maps that you can compare with your OS map to get more detail. The photographs in this book are all taken by me and, as the countryside itself has no copyright, there is no case to answer there.

The information presented in this book is correct to the best of my knowledge at the time of writing but, if you find an error or difference of opinion, it will add to the interest of your day.

Many of the fields are occupied by cows and sheep. It is vital that any gates are left as you find them and, that will usually be shut. The invention of hinges and fastenings was well known 4000 years ago and examples have been found in ancient Egypt. The technology has only recently arrived around Penybont and most gates are still fastened up with binder twine rather than operating properly. Also, it is important that if you take a dog with you, that it is kept under proper and safe control. That means keeping on a lead when near farm animals.

Penybont Inn

There is a public house in Penybont on the junction between the B4396 and the lane to Llansantfraid. Some public houses are called So and So Arms. Some are just called by a name. Others are called The So and So. This one is called Penybont Inn. I don't know why it's an Inn and not an Arms but we'll let it be. There is a car park for the Inn but, it is impolite to use it just for walking. If you intend to use the Inn afterwards, still ask first, that's nice and decent.

There used to be two Inns in Penybont. The existing Inn is just Penybont Inn. The newer of the two was called the New Inn and it's now a private house. It was a busy place at one time because it had a railway station that went up the Tanat valley and connected its inhabitants to the rest of the country. People stopped using the railway a lot and the service got chopped. It wasn't anything to do with the Beeching cuts if that's what you were thinking. It was some years earlier. While we are on the subject, it's worth mentioning that Beeching was just the hatchet man drafted in to chop the railways up. The real criminal was the transport minister whose fortune was in road haulage and he didn't want the railways. He eventually fled to Spain when his behaviour came to light. There he lived out his days after all the damage and corruption he was responsible for had been done. There was no extradition in those days. It would be lovely to have steam locomotives contentedly puffing their way up the Tanat Valley but these days the only thing puffing round here is you, especially on the hilly bits.

I hope that you have a happy time exploring Penybont and the surrounding area.

In Penybont you can expect unusual sights. Here's a couple:

A night sky above Penybont

Sunset at Penybont

Walk 1 – Highland Lane Inner Loop

3 miles. Uphill for the first half and downhill on the way back.

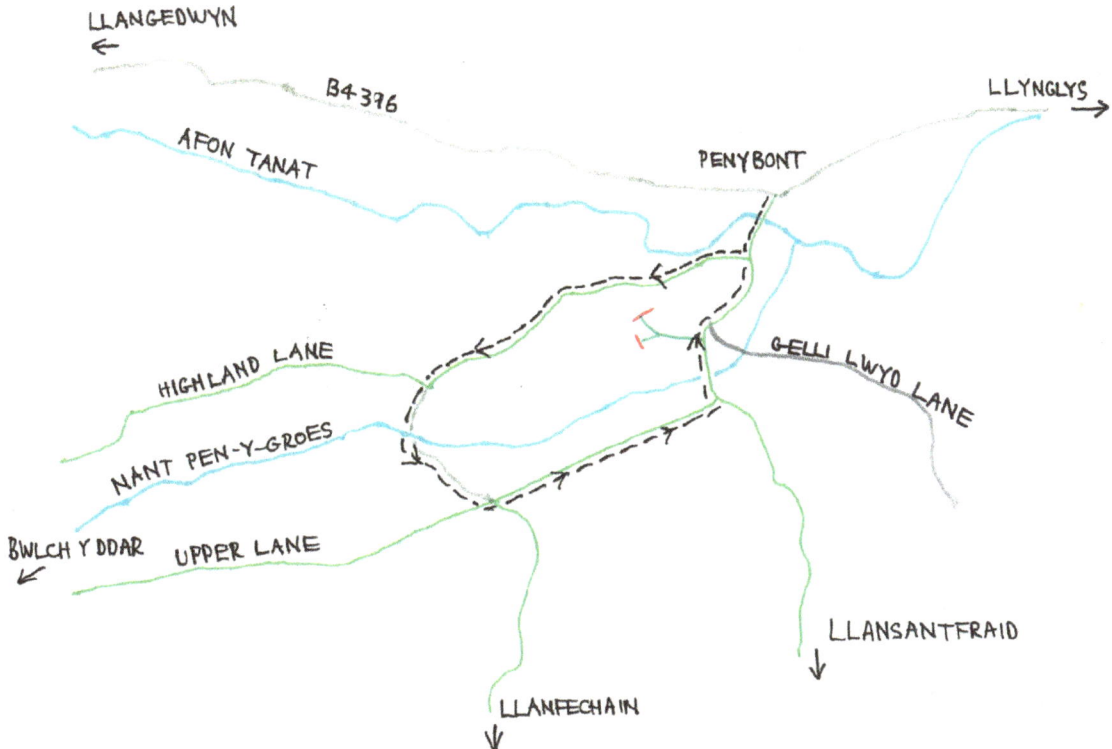

LLANGEDWYN

B4 376

AFON TANAT

LLYNGLYS

PENYBONT

HIGHLAND LANE

GELLI LWYD LANE

NANT PEN-Y-GROES

BWLCH Y DDAR   UPPER LANE

LLANSANTFRAID

LLANFECHAIN

Map is about 2.5 inches to a mile with the walk shown as a dashed line.
This walk takes about two hours, including time to enjoy views, fauna and flora.

Walk down the Llansantfraid lane from the B4396. Cross the Tanat using the Penybont Bridge. Pause in the centre to admire the upstream view. Look down into the river. If it's calm, you may see trout using their muscles to stay in line with the flow while they watch for flies. Cross over and admire the downstream river while it cackles over the rocks. If it has rained heavily before your visit, you will simply see a lot of muddy water going under the bridge.

Continue to the first bend where on the right you will see the site of the old coal yard which used to be Penybont Station. It was called Llansilin Road Station but is now a building site on the next step in Penybont's development.

Immediately after the building site, turn right up Highland Lane. On the right you will follow a Yew hedge that thankfully remains though it has been cut. I hope that this lovely hedge continues. It used to provide shelter for the people standing on the station platform and, in common with all hedges, provides a secure nesting site for birds and a haven for other wildlife. On the left is a field often sown with maize for cattle feed.

At the end of the Yew hedge on the right is a gate and an area of woodland and, you will see the track bed of the old Tanat Valley railway. It would be lovely to see a train, contentedly chuffing its way up the valley through the trees. We will only ever see that vision in our mind's eye. The fact is that the men who worked hard to achieve that railway are long gone, replaced by generations that have little interest in a national rail system that provides every community with a link to the network. Progress today is more about making money than serving the community. We dry our eyes and walk on.

The level walk that may have given you a false sense of ease, starts to climb and wind upwards. Once you have gone round the bend, (the one on the lane I mean), the view to the right will begin to open up. If you look to the right you will see the village of Penybont. Below you flows the Tanat River. Across the river are hills. The predominant one is Gyrn Moelfre. Most locals just call it "The Gyrn". There are other Gyrns but, for our locality there is just this one. It is the mountain on the right hand side of the following photograph. It has a long gradual slope from right to left up to the summit and a much steeper slope to the left. The farm buildings below The Gyrn are the epicentre of muck spreading for the whole area. Here the spreaders are refilled from a huge lagoon of slurry. In the centre of the photograph is a white building on the junction of the B4396 with the lane to Llansilin. This is the Green Inn, another popular public house.

Eventually, you stop climbing when you reach Belan Cottage on the left. On the right is a gate over which you may savour the northward view *(overleaf)*.

After another three hundred yards you come to a track on the left. This is your route. You will know you have reached the right place because there is a defunct JCB in the field to the right of the track opening. This is a fixture that fits the normal farm practice of letting failed machinery weather slowly into agricultural sculptures. It's quite nice really, forming a nesting site for the birds and a haven for insect life.

A sign ahead tells you that the descent is steep. It certainly is. Take your time and admire the scenery on the way down. At the bottom is the stream called Nant Pen-y-Groes. You can either

Northward view from Highland lane, including The Gyrn

plod through it if the water is low or, you can cross by the footbridge to your left. On the right hand side across the stream, there are often a few Highland cattle, sometimes referred to as Longhorns. Indeed the horns are very prominent but, they are most genial animals and it is lovely to see them with their bull, George. Follow the track gently upwards until you come to the lane by a farm and haulage company. Follow the lane to a crossroads. Straight over is a lane to Llanfechain but, you turn left here. Follow the lane downhill. It is very straight and I believe that it must be on the bed of a Roman road. Welsh or English people never make roads straight. Even today, the Highways Agency plans lots of bends to remove any possibility that you could safely overtake. The emphasis these days is to make journeys as inefficient and long lasting as possible. As a child, I was allocated a small patch of garden in which I constructed baffles and deviations for my Corgi and Dinky models. After a few short years, I matured and acquired long trousers and a job. My interest in giving my toy cars a hard time waned. The Highways Agency appears to be a bunch of people that haven't taken that step to maturity. Their aim remains to give a hard time to the motorist. The Romans conquered Britain except for Scotland over two thousand years ago. They taught civilisation including road building, central heating, washing and organisation in general. When they left, the locals couldn't wait to get back to crooked roads, shoddy building practices and disorganisation. Hence we entered the dark ages which have persisted ever since. Anyway, we digress.

Follow the lane downhill with care. It is quiet but you need to keep an eye and ear open for traffic. To the left is the view across the Nant Pen-y-Groes valley to the hills on Highland Lane. After a while, the views open up towards Penybont village. To the right is a hill called Berwyn; not to be confused with the Berwyn Mountains that are a few miles further west. Our own little Berwyn is important as it is the only hill in the vicinity with a triangulation point on top and offers stunning views all round and alignment with other triangulation points on the national network.

Eventually you arrive at a T junction with the Penybont to Llansantfraid road. This road is much busier and frequented by drivers who have an inbuilt feeling of invincibility. There can be no other explanation for the high speed with which they travel on this single track road with all its blind bends and humps. Turn left and walk back to Penybont. Take care and listen for approaching vehicles.

You descend to Nant Pen-y-groes which you cross on the road bridge. On the left is a derelict chapel that was built in 1812 and enlarged in 1858 and is a testimony to days when worship was nearly universal in Britain, especially in Wales where every hamlet had its chapel.

This chapel now lies derelict with hardly any roof, awaiting renovation or probably conversion to housing.

The lane is particularly narrow at this point so care is needed.

There were no motor vehicles when this building was erected!

Penygroes Chapel

Continuing past chicken sheds on both sides of the road, you come to the T junction with Highland Lane that you ascended earlier in the walk.

Crossing Nany Penygroes on track from Highland Lane

Llansantfraid to Penybont Lane
Penybont in background to right. The Gyrn straight ahead

Thus ends stroll number one. I hope you enjoyed it and feel motivated to return to Penybont and try the other walks described in this book.

Walk 2 – Highland Lane Outer Loop

8 miles. Uphill for the first half and downhill on the way back.

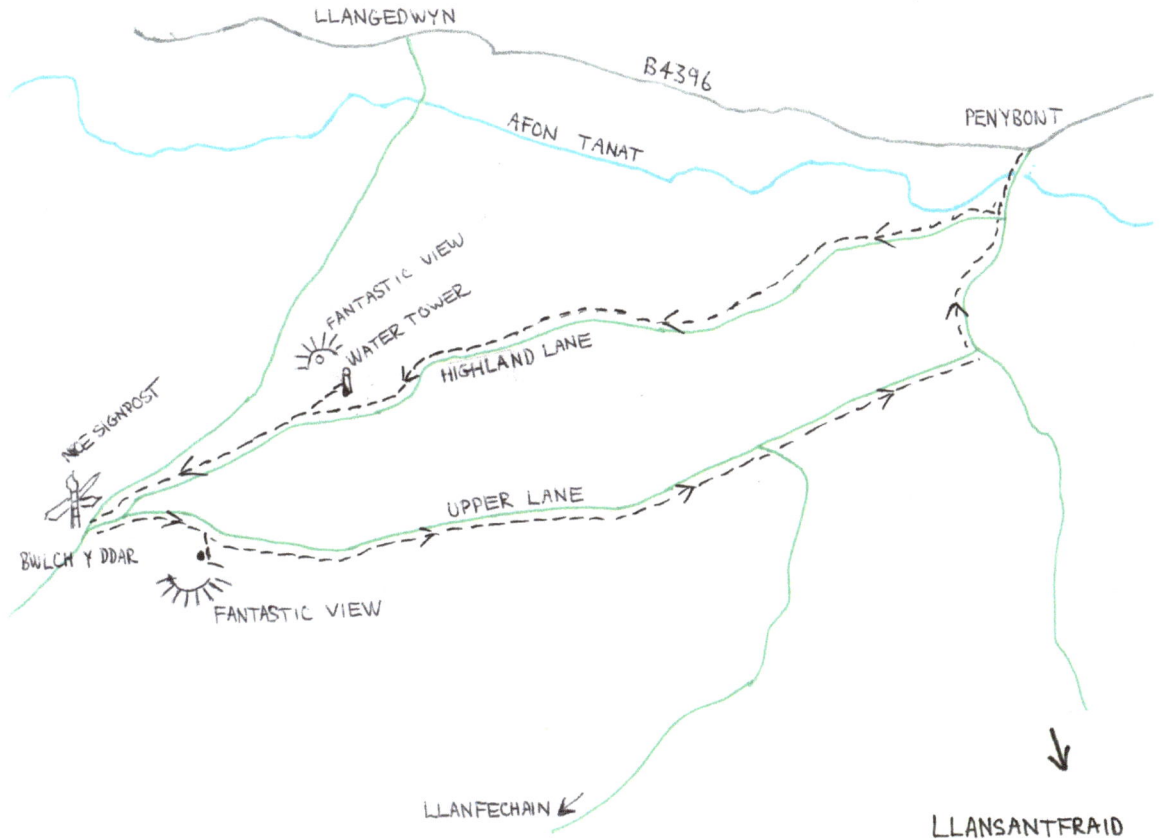

Map is about 2.5 inches to a mile with the walk shown as a dashed line.
This walk takes about four hours, including time to enjoy views, fauna and flora

Proceed from Penybont as Walk 1 up to the retired JCB where you turned left down the track to Nant Penygroes. This time, you don't turn left: you carry straight on. You go round a sort of curving straight and begin to climb again but, don't worry because the climb is short and then you are on the top.

Look to the left and across the Nant Penygroes valley you will pick out your return walk on the hillside. Look left further and you will see the Breidden Hills with Rodney's Pillar standing atop the main hump. The Admiral Rodney was an admirable chap by all accounts and well respected by his community and men. They erected the pillar to commemorate his naval victories. I don't suppose it cost much to build but apparently the local officials believe that it needs fixing and the cost will be £160,000 to replace the stolen lightning conductor and repair a crack in the structure! The north side of the Breiddens that you are looking at bear a huge scar due to quarrying activity.

Continuing another few yards, you see our reservoir on the right. Normally, a reservoir is not on top of a hill because it needs water to feed into it from surrounding streams. This reservoir has water pumped up to it and the height provides the head of pressure to supply the local communities. The reservoir is an underground tank. The most amusing thing about this site is the number of warning signs fixed to its gates. When I first came up here in 2019, there were thirteen warning signs fixed to the gates. Evidently, some official at Hafren Dyfrdwy loves rules and regulations. There was even one telling you not to drive at more than thirteen miles per hour on the site which is a small compound about ten yards long. Most of the signs have now been nicked or broken off by people who realised they looked daft. Such signage appears to be an evidence of what corporate management is like: dictatorial, wanting to control your every breath, wasteful and largely unnecessary. It is nice to turn on the tap and expect water to come out which it often does. However, the cost of delivering a product that simply pours out of the sky, is high and explained by excessive overheads.

After another few yards you come to Highland Farm where you will usually see some of the herd of Dexter Cattle. They are lovely gentle animals. After the farm you climb for about fifty yards and you will see a track on the right. Just walk a few yards up the track to a gate. You will be rewarded by a wonderful view across the Tanat valley and to the left, the Berwyn Mountains. When you have taken your fill of the view, return down the track to Highland Lane.

Continue up the lane, enjoying views to the left. You will see the lane for the return journey on the opposite hillside. Occasional views to the Breiddens open up. After a time, you will reach a straight level walk with wonderful views to the right across the Tanat valley to The Gyrn and the Berwyn Mountains to the left. Straight ahead you see a hill with a water tower on top. In another few minutes, the tower is on your right and, having passed it, you see a stile. There is no obligation to do so but, it is worth crossing the stile and walking up to the tower. The 360^0 view is stunning. To the west lie the Berwyns. North is The Gyrn. East is The Wrekin. Southeast are the Breiddens.

Northwest from near the water tower

The Gyrn and Llangedwyn from the water tower

Retrace your steps to Highland Lane and continue past pine woods that were significantly harvested in 2021 but, thankfully, many trees remain. After the woodland, further excellent views across the Tanat valley can be enjoyed until you reach Bwlch y Ddar village. Although you don't have to, it is worth walking down to the village crossroads. There is no cake shop but, there is a lovely old signpost on the crossroads that so far, the highways department has not replaced with the inelegant erections they spoil the countryside with today.

Bwlch is nothing to do with size: it's a small village. It means "pass" and is at the summit of the pass from Llangedwyn to Llanfyllin. I don't know what the Ddar bit means. It may be a proper name or it may refer to an oak tree. If I find anyone old enough to tell me, I'll let you know later. Having appreciated the sign from yesteryear, return to the Y fork and take the right hand limb. Just when you thought there was no more climbing, there is a steep but short rise to the summit.

Signpost at Bwlch y Ddar

The view left to the Berwyns is beautiful. A little further on you will see a large gate on the right and a stunning view southwards towards mid Wales. On a clear day you can see the wind farm on the summit of Llandinam. If you cross the field, which is not a public footpath, you will be rewarded with a better view southwards. The village of Llanfechain lies below you and, on a clear day, the whole vista takes some time to absorb so allow it to penetrate and better the mind. You return an improved and more wholesome being. Like proper music that works on your brain through your ears, a vista like this works on your brain through your eyes and does its job. The chemist gives you pills to treat symptoms. Nature gives you a view to treat the cause. You get stressed with all sorts of nastiness but views like this sooth and bring peace. Let's call it the "healing view". Sit on the rise and, if you've been wise enough to remember your hip flask, enjoy a dram with your sandwich.

The Breiddens and Llanfechain from the "healing view"

Continue down the lane. It appears not to be named so, for the purpose of identification, I call it "Upper Lane". It runs fairly parallel to Highland Lane but on a higher level. After a few bends, you will notice that it becomes dead straight. This tells us that it was built by the Romans as British people, even now, refuse to make straight roads. They prefer bendy ones. Straight roads have all the advantages of better visibility, shorter distance and increased safety. However, those concepts need sense to perceive and sense has apparently not yet percolated the heads of those who have any say in our highways planning.

Enjoy the straight descent of Upper Lane until you arrive at the crossroads attained in Walk 1 where the track arrives from Highland Lane. From here you follow the same route as Walk 1 back to Penybont.

Walk 3 – Highland Lane and Railway

5 miles. Uphill for the first half and downhill on the way back.

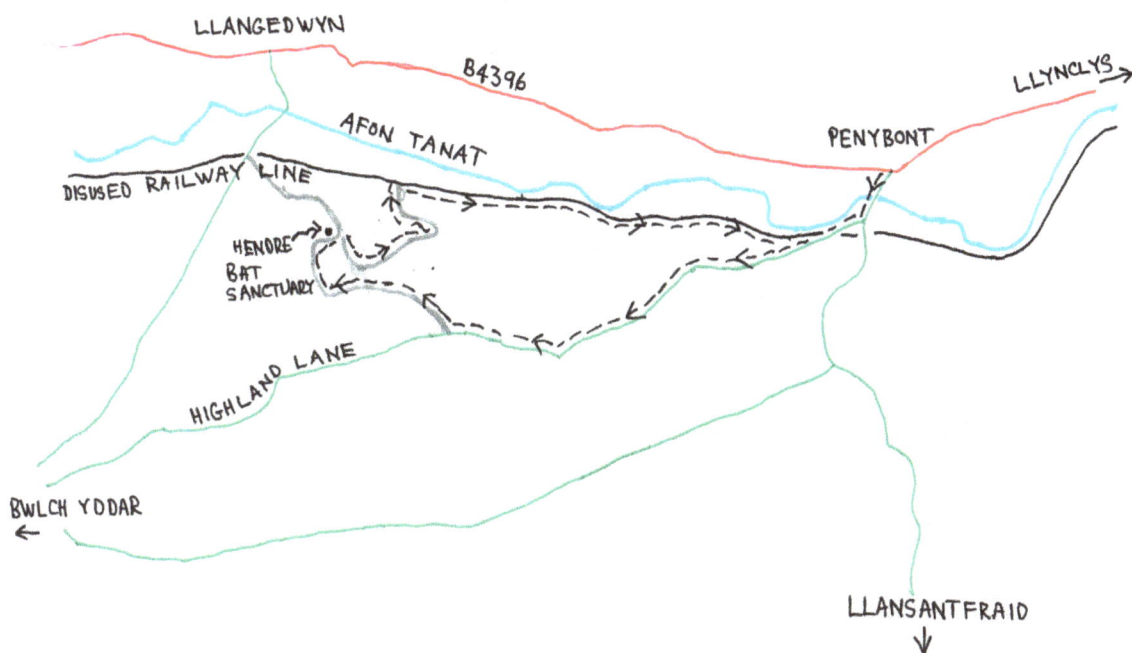

LLANGEDWYN

B4396

LLYNCLYS →

AFON TANAT

PENYBONT

DISUSED RAILWAY LINE

HENDRE
BAT
SANCTUARY

HIGHLAND LANE

BWLCH YODAR
←

LLANSANTFRAID
↓

Map is about 2.5 inches to a mile with the walk shown as a dashed line.
This walk takes about three hours, including time to enjoy views, fauna and flora.

ollow the route of Walk 2 as far as the track on the right after Highland Farm. This time you take that track which is a public highway. You can drive down it in your car but, unless it's one of the Chelsea Tractors that many people like today, you won't make it. Even if you could make it, taking cars down this track spoils it for nature lovers so, let's walk.

The scenery is very pretty. At first, you enjoy views across the Tanat valley to the hills beyond. After a while you enter larch woodland. The larch is our only deciduous pine. It has lovely delicate foliage in summer but until then, you will get views through the woods. April is a nice time to visit because the bluebells are in flower.

At the bottom of the woods you cross a stream and continue past a house that is now a bat sanctuary, to a stile on the right.

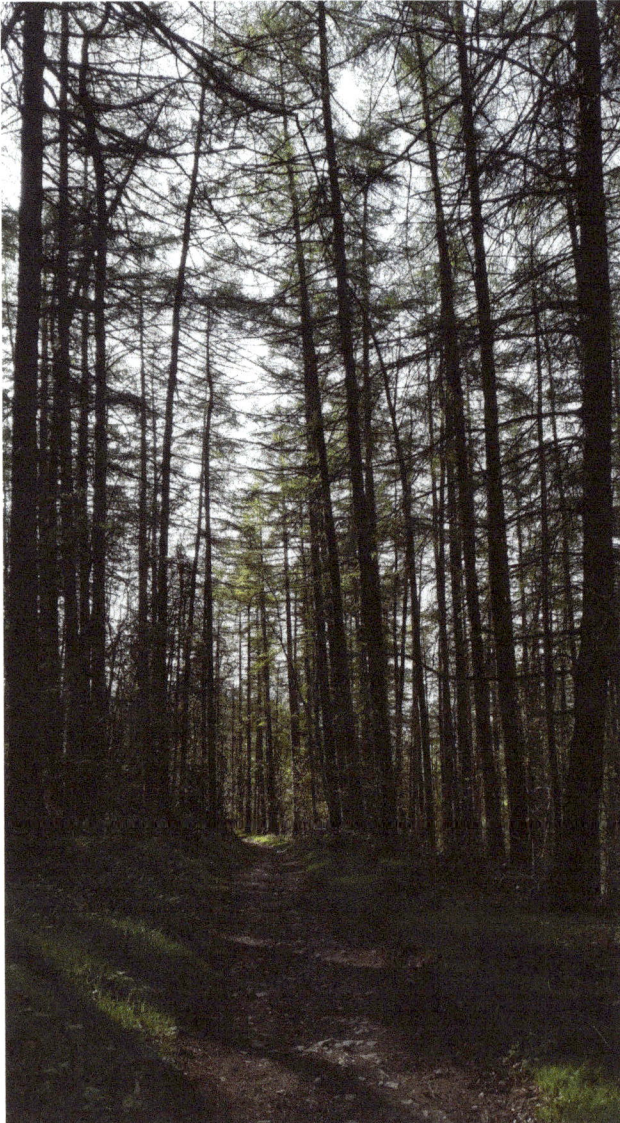

That it is a public footpath is seen by the remains of a way sign nailed to it. All that is left now are the four nails with a bit of yellow plastic under each one. Anyway, you cross the stile and head down the track to the stream again. Cross with care because it's a bit squelchy.

Then head up to the field. As you enter the field there is a complete public footpath sign. Cross the field diagonally downwards to a gate that you will see in the far corner. Through the gate which I don't think is a public footpath, is a track that leads down to a T junction. At the junction you turn left and, follow the track steeply downwards until you arrive at a gate.

After the gate, continue for a few yards until you reach the railway track bed.

Track through the larch woods

Again this is not a public footpath, but is used regularly for walks. One village member who was challenged over walking on it has written to the estate owner and received a positive reply, allowing walking and as long as gates are shut and nature is respected, there is no problem to walking on the route of the old railway. After all, a few humans are not doing any more damage than a chuffing train. Anyway, you follow the old railway line back to Penybont.

Occasionally, there are cows on the track and there are sometimes electric fences to contain them. An electric fence between your legs gives incredible sensations and is not to be recommended. The correct procedure is to carefully step over or lie on the ground and roll under the live wire. As long as you are a few inches clear of the wire, you will not use any electricity. Always leave gates exactly as you find them. Enjoy the Tanat as it burbles its way downstream.

When you near Penybont, a final gate catch is a bent peg that fits through a chain. Immediately after this gate is a path on the right leading up to Highland Lane. From there you turn left follow the lane back to Penybont as in Walk 2.

The old railway line towards Penybont

Hendre bat sanctuary

Gravel Hill from railway line

Walk 4 – Winllan Hill

5 miles. Uphill for the first half and downhill on the way back.

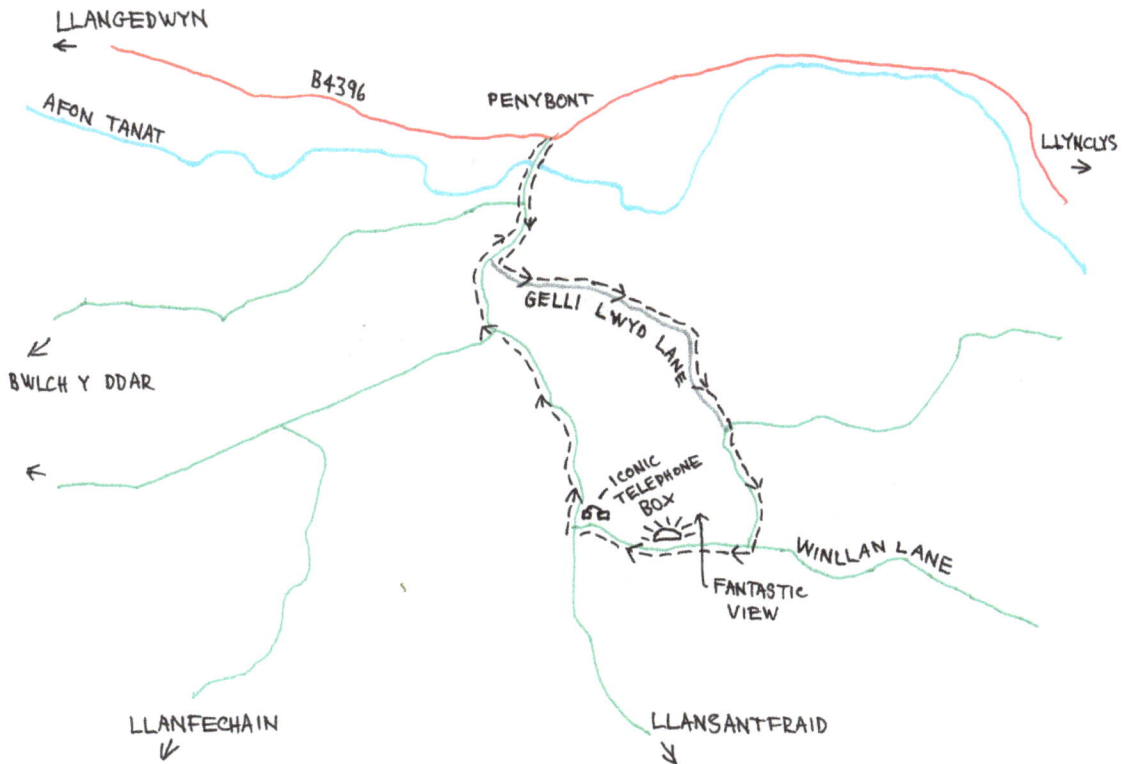

LLANGEDWYN

B4396

PENYBONT

AFON TANAT

LLYNCLYS

BWLCH Y DDAR

GELLI LWYD LANE

ICONIC TELEPHONE BOX

WINLLAN LANE

FANTASTIC VIEW

LLANFECHAIN

LLANSANTFRAID

Map is about 2.5 inches to a mile with the walk shown as a dashed line.
This walk takes about three hours, including time to enjoy views, fauna and flora.

From Penybont centre, follow the lane towards Llansantfraid. First you cross Penybont Bridge and continue past the old coal yard that was formerly Llansilin Road Station and is now a building site for housing. Continue past the Highland Lane turning. The Llansantfraid Lane is narrow and bendy and at times, busy. Keep your eyes and ears tuned to the signs of approaching vehicles, especially for ones being driven with a high degree of madness that is common to this area. Always remember that pulling yourself up the hedge may be undignified but, it's better than lying under the wheels of a vehicle.

After a few hundred yards you come to chicken sheds on both sides of the road. Immediately after the sheds, turn left. There is a sign that is somewhat mobile, being a little board that lies on its back on the verge. It is marked Ty Bryn Ochr. Bryn means hill and Ochr means side. This relates to the house of this name on the lane.

The lane down which you are walking is called Gelli Lwyd Lane. Gelli means copse and Lwyd generally means grey so, the person naming this lane must have wanted people to think of grey woods. To me, woods are brown, but green when the leaves are on the trees. That is, unless the trees are silver birch when the term grey could loosely be applied. Silver birches are not so common here and, it's doubtful if that's the explanation. We have to leave the interpretation with the fertile mind of the one doing the naming and I guess we will never really know. There's always people with strongly voiced opinions but, in my experience they usually fall into the category of those who don't know, but try to make it sound convincing. Anyway, we digress. The useful thing is that someone named this lane and that's nice for identification purposes. Most lanes round here are not named officially. People who live here name them but, the nouns are only known to their immediate contacts. They rarely make it to the Ordnance Survey maps.

After a couple of hundred yards you come to a newish house on the right. There are generally two or three dogs in the garden that have an awful lot to say for themselves when you approach. Sometimes the volume and its suddenness can make you jump if they haven't spotted you until the last minute. I'm only telling you this so that you are aware of the noise before you experience it.

Immediately after the house with the dogs the lane becomes a track. You continue on the track which offers pretty views on both sides. Winllan Hill opens up on your right and the hills on the far side of the Tanat are on your left. Winllan means vineyard but I wouldn't spend much time looking for grapes. I've never see one here except in a packet. Optimism isn't a bad thing but if you overdo it, it just leads to disappointment and it would be a pity to waste a nice day looking for vines on this hill.

After a steady but bendy climb you arrive at a summit which is surmounted by a tree that looks as if it has endured a strong wind throughout its life. Stop here for a while and turn round because the view is worth it. You can see the Berwyn Mountains in the background and nearer at hand, the Gyrn and many other hills.

Gelli Lwyd Lane where the tarmac gives way to a track

Summit of Gelli Lwyd Lane looking West

Continue along Gelli Lwyd Lane, enjoying the sights, sounds and those good old country smells and the humming flies attracted by them. After about half a mile, you come to a T junction with a tarmac lane. If you turned left you would go to Llanyblodwel but you don't turn left. You turn right and this takes you eventually to Winllan summit. First, you go steeply downhill which brings the inevitable consequence that you will go steeply uphill to get to the top.

After the down and up, the lane levels off a bit and a track on the left leads to a farm. If you stop here and look over the gate on the left of this track, there is a lovely view to The Gyrn and other hills.

Continue gently uphill for a few hundred yards until you reach a T junction with Winllan Lane. In the opposite hedge is a nice bench seat that was purchased and placed there by a local villager who thought it would be a good place for walkers to rest after climbing the hill. What a lovely thoughtful act and one that has brought a lot of pleasure.

Next to the bench is a stile that can only be seen when the hedge is not in leaf. For some reason, the stile and footpath are unavailable unless you take secateurs to remove the hedge from around it. The footpath from the stile would take you to Plas Onn and onward to Llansantfraid. The footpath is marked on the latest OS maps. From the bench you walk up Winllan Lane, admiring to views on the right to The Gyrn and many other hills as far as the Berwyn Mountains. In the centre of the view lies Penybont village. Continue along Winllan Lane until you reach a telephone kiosk.

The bench on Winllan Lane and occluded stile

Telephone kiosk, Winllan Lane

This delightful structure reminds you, if you are old enough, of the days before mobile phones. In those days there was a phone in this box that was connected to the national network. If you needed to make a call, you had to walk to this device and dial your number and feed it with coins. Well there's no phone in it now. You can adopt the box for nothing to establish a village library in it, or to put a defibrillator in it. However, if you want it in your garden, you have to buy one for thousands of pounds. In fact, you can buy ten nice sheds for the price of one of these. Where it stands doesn't merit a defib, or a library. So, there it stands, forlorn though not unloved; until someone with thousands to spare, keeps the racket going and gets it transplanted into their garden to keep the spade and fork in. It has become popular to house defibs in these boxes. This satisfies the philanthropic activity of local communities and is well pleasing to the defib suppliers.

The truth is that defibs are surprisingly not often useful for saving lives. If you happen to have one of the shockable rhythms, and someone nearby knows how to use the device, then happy days: a life has been spared to die of something else later on. But if the heart has stopped or is about to, the defib records the event and does nothing to help you. It isn't designed to restart a heart. It is designed to reset a very small number of abnormal rhythms. The most valuable heart aid you can learn is cardiopulmonary resuscitation, abbreviated like everything these days to an acronym, CPR. It's a posh way of saying, squish the heart a few times and get some air in the lungs. The simple things are usually the best. This is a good first aid procedure to learn. You never know when it will come in handy. If you know the ropes and have practiced it well on a dummy, (they don't normally let you practice it on healthy people), you can save a life. But you might not find many candidates for your skill on the corner of Winllan Lane. Long may this be the case. We don't want a city here, thank you.

You leave the telephone kiosk behind, together with the reminiscence of the day when you rang your auntie Mildred and spent half an hour and five bob of your hard earned money to discuss her chilblains. You arrive after a few yards, at the T junction with the lane from Penybont to Llansantffraid. You turn right and make your way downhill to Penybont. You take care because the lane is busy and bendy and some of the drivers are unfit to use wheelbarrows, let alone vehicles with engines. The only way they could have passed their driving test is because the examiner didn't want to see them again.

Continue down the lane and when you get as far as the T junction with Upper Lane, you follow Walk 2 back to Penybont. This return leg is quite nice as it is all downhill and therefore easy. It affords decent views of Penybont village and the hills beyond.

Walk 5 – Llanyblodwel

8 miles. Mainly level but, uphill for the first half of the return journey.

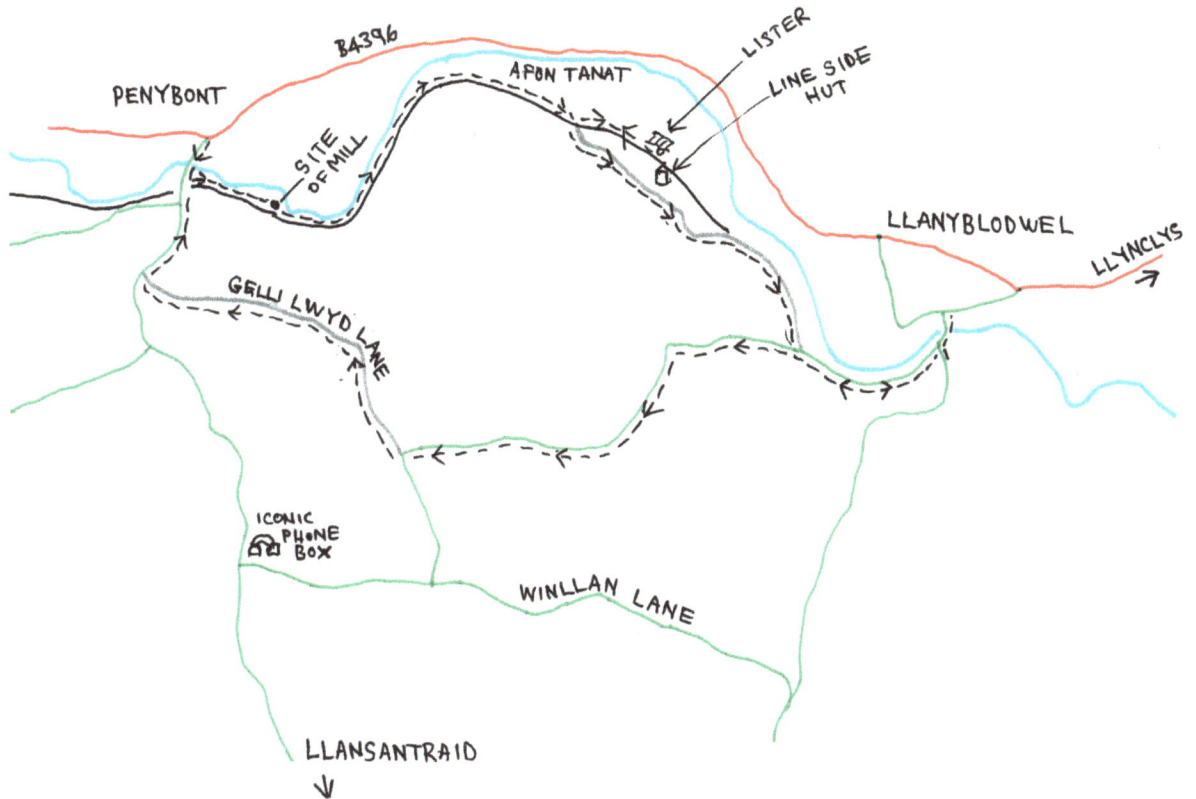

Map is about 2.5 inches to a mile with the walk shown as a dashed line.
This walk takes about four hours, including time to enjoy views, fauna and flora.

rom Penybont centre, follow the lane towards Llansantfraid. Immediately after crossing the Tanat there is a lane on the left to the New Inn that is now a private house. Turn left at the back of the first house. After the house there is a gate on the right. Through the gate there is a track that you follow round a long curving straight across a field and down to the Nant Pen-y-groes stream. You wobble across the stream on a few loose stones. If you are good at this sort of thing, you will comfortably manage it. If the stream is in spate and you are unsteady, it's still quite safe but you will spend the rest of the walk in wet socks. This is the point at which the Nant Pen-y-groes flows into the Tanat.

After crossing the stream, you walk through the next field in a diagonal manner up to the far right hand corner. In this field there are often two or three herons resting in the long grass. They will startle you as they rise into the air on their huge grey wings. You appreciate their size when you are up close. At the corner of the field you go through a gate and you are on the old railway line. There is no need to listen for trains. The last one passed in 1951 so, unless your hearing is unusually acute, you've missed it. Turn left and follow the line, or rather, the line of the line.

There are a few gates and a couple of bridges to cross. Most of the woodwork on the bridges has rotted so you need to be careful. Either climb down and up the other side or, gingerly stay on the main beams that span the gap. The walk along the railway track bed provides many lovely views of Afon Tanat on the left and Winllan Hill on the right.

Along railway track bed towards Llanyblodwel

After about half a mile, you come to a track feeding in from the left. This track comes from the B4396, crossing the Tanat by means of a footbridge just east of a layby. This is worth a look if you haven't seen it before. I have walked twice along the B4396 from Penybont and crossed the Tanat by this footbridge. The time I did this was during Boris Johnson's first lockdown. That was the time when nearly all the nation feared to leave their front door unless it was for a trip to the Supermarket which incongruously, they believed was safe compared with visits elsewhere. It is a fact that politicians know that if they want nonsense to be believed, all they have to do is repeat it over and over again with a straight face, or preferably, get an "expert" to do so. The B4396 was quiet and relatively safe during the first lockdown. The police positioned check points here and there to see if people had legitimate reason to be out and about. Of course, ministers and their advisors were doing their own thing. One of them went from London to Doncaster to seek childcare and to check his eyesight while he had Covid. Other top flight ministers partied away the hours and celebrated birthdays in London, but before all that got widely known, the provinces were eerily quiet and the B4396 was for once safe. Subsequent lockdowns were not regarded with the same respect and the roads were as busy as ever during the day, travelled by all those on furlough who were working from home when they had done their own things. Suffice it to say that the B4396 has no pavement and is very busy with hundreds of huge farm vehicles and heavy lorries and cars per hour, making it utterly unsafe to walk along, even with a High Vis jacket and a tin hat.

Anyway, we digress. Getting back to the intersection of the track from the footbridge, you carry on for another few yards on the railway bed until the footpath forks off to the right. If you are interested in history, you should carry on for about 30 yards on the railway track. There is a lineside hut on the right and you can't get inside because a huge tree has grown in front of the door. But, you can get the door open enough to see where the workers made their tea. Everything is pretty much as they left it when they finished their last shift in 1951 although some freight apparently continued until 1964. Opposite the hut is a Lister elevator. This is a relic from the days when potato harvesting was a manual activity. The Lister elevated the crop into a lorry or trailer and was loaded by hand.

Following the footpath from the railway, you soon arrive at a farm. A notice warns you that cows and calves are loose. People worry about cows but they eat them whereas cows don't eat people. Cows are herbivores and if they do have a go at you, it won't be with the intention of converting you to a meal. Cows are like many animals. They live to eat and reproduce and like chewing the cud in a contented fashion. Few creatures apart from human beings will attack for the fun of it. Cows are good mums and don't take kindly to you messing with their babies. As long as you leave well alone and don't get between the cow and the baby, all will be absolutely fine. You walk through the farm, keeping to the track. There is a cattle grid to cross either side of the farm.

After the farm, you continue along the farm lane towards Llanyblodwel until you reach the minor road. I recommend that you turn left here and walk into Llanyblodwel which is a beautiful village. The first building you come to on the left is Crossing Cottage and you will see the evidence that the railway crossed the road at this point and continued to Llanyblodwel on the right side of the road.

When you reach the centre of the village you will see a number of lovely buildings including the Horseshoes Pub. This was a thriving establishment. Opposite the Pub is the stone bridge over the Tanat and is a beautiful structure. It is worth getting down to the water on the downstream side of the bridge and looking up at the arch. It really is a fine piece of engineering and admirably suited to the needs of its year. They would never have expected farm machinery bigger than houses, driven in a rush by folk with short fuses.

The beautiful stone bridge over the Tanat is a listed structure and rightly so. It is listed in two senses as I write these words. Farming tends to be what we might loosely call a rustic process and in 2021, I'm told that one of the farm operatives crashed his tractor and trailer into the bridge. As a result it is closed to traffic until the council find the money and inclination to fix it. On the B4396 east of the turn to Llanyblodwel, a large notice has been placed, declaring the bridge closed to traffic for "urgent" repairs. Nine months later at the time of writing, there is no sign of work starting. When I learned the meaning of words at school, "urgent" conveyed the idea of a matter that needed attending to with speed. Shropshire Highways department presumably has a more relaxed understanding of the adjective. Until this council gets round to it, the inhabitants of Llanyblodwell living south of the bridge have a fraught journey over the Winllan to get to the rest of Britain. Seeing that the bridge was built in 1710 and Shropshire council took it over in 1899, it's high time that this body of people stopped imbibing Camellia Sinensis and got on with the job. After all, in 1710, the bridge was built with no power tools in a shorter time than the council has spent thinking about fixing it, and at considerably less cost in real and relative terms.

The Crossroads Cottage

The Horseshoes Inn
Llanyblodwel Bridge

When you have absorbed the village and watched the river passing under the bridge, and thought about it awhile, you walk back up the lane to where the farm lane joined it. You might still be thinking of the water as you walk up the road. A number of mills drew their power from the Tanat. You can't use the power up. It flows on to the next mill. But in relation to any one mill, you cannot grind with the water that is past. These words have been attributed to various folk but the earliest reference I could find was of George Herbert in 1651. How true it is that we should use each moment as an opportunity. You carry on up the road. When you get to the first bend, stop and look backwards. There is a fine view to the village. It's quite a pull up the hill and you will need to stop for a minute anyway. After a few more bends the view opens up to the right across and up the Tanat valley. Continue past a farm and onwards until you see a good view of the Winllan Hill on the left.

A little further on you will see a property on the right with a tree house in the front garden. Just after this, you will see the turning on the right that is Gelli Lwyd Lane. You turn right here and follow the lane back to Penybont. You walked this lane in the reverse order in Walk 4.

Llanyblodwel from lane to Winllan Hill

Walk 6 – Berwyn

4 miles. Uphill steeply for the first half and downhill on the return.

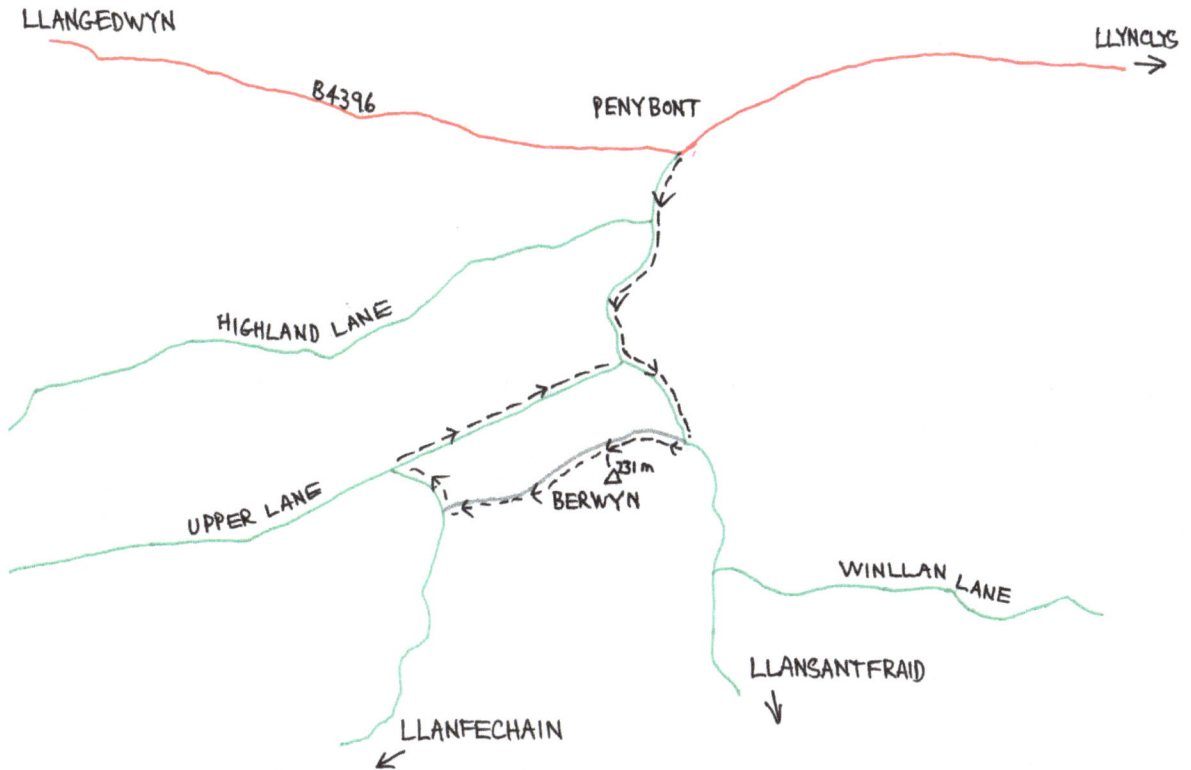

Map is about 2.5 inches to a mile with the walk shown as a dashed line.
This walk takes about three hours, including time to enjoy views, fauna and flora.

From various vantage points you can see the trig point on the top of Berwyn. For anything to have a trig point, there is significance in its position and generally, the view from the trig point is wonderful. At 231m, Berwyn is not a mountain and folk have built chimneys higher than that in Britain. However, the view from the top is marvellous in all directions. Throughout time, high points have been attractive for the views provided. Years ago, people used hills as beacons from which to transmit messages up and down the country. They tried mirrors but although that worked on sunny days, there weren't enough of them to offer reliable messaging so, they resorted to lighting fires. We aren't sure how the fire was interpreted. Just lighting a fire would enable the next beacon to detect the light but what was being conveyed? Had someone got married, or died or, was there an invasion? Perhaps they used blankets to block the signal periodically in a Morse code type arrangement. Suffice it to say that it apparently worked and was probably about as reliable as the current British mobile signal network. Anyway, whether you wish to practice semaphore or just enjoy the spectacular view, the walk is well worthwhile. It is best to do it on a nice day. In a thick mist or a thunderstorm, it's less attractive.

From Penybont centre, you cross the Afon Tanat by means of the road bridge. Continue past the first and second right turns to Bwlch y Ddar. Be careful along this road as it is busy and driven on regularly by folk of impatience and low talent. After a few hundred yards you notice the spine of Berwyn on your right and there is a gate. There is no signed footpath up Berwyn but, the path is clearly marked on the Ordnance Survey map. Through the gate, I follow the hedge uphill. This line takes you round the north side of the hill and, when you come to a break in the hedge on your left, you walk through and up to the trig point.

There the view through 360^0 is fantastic. To the north the predominant feature is Gyrn Moelfre. The southerly views display the mid Wales hills. The Breidden hills are close by to the southeast. In the distance to the east you can see the Wrekin.

Gyrn Moelfre from Berwyn

The Wrekin from Berwyn

Penybont from Berwyn

Continue west following the Berwyn ridge. The views are nice all the way. Eventually, you reach the hedge bordering the road from Upper Lane to Llanfechain. Turn right and follow the hedge down to Upper Lane. Through the gate you can walk down Upper Lane until you reach the junction with the road to Penybont. Turn left and walk carefully back to the village.

Berwyn is normally inhabited by sheep and you need to ensure that all gates are properly fastened and that you leave nothing behind apart from footprints.

Though you will always attend to this need, it is vital for the welfare of the livestock and the goodwill of the landowners.

Walking back along Upper Lane you will keep looking up at the flanks of Berwyn. Though not a Munroe, it is a lovely walk and one that many people have not done, but now you have. If you live to have white hair, which is what Berwyn means, you will still remember the day you climbed it with fond memories.

Berwyn Trig Point

Walk 7 – Gyrn Moelfre (The Gyrn)

6 miles. Uphill steeply for the first half and downhill on the return.

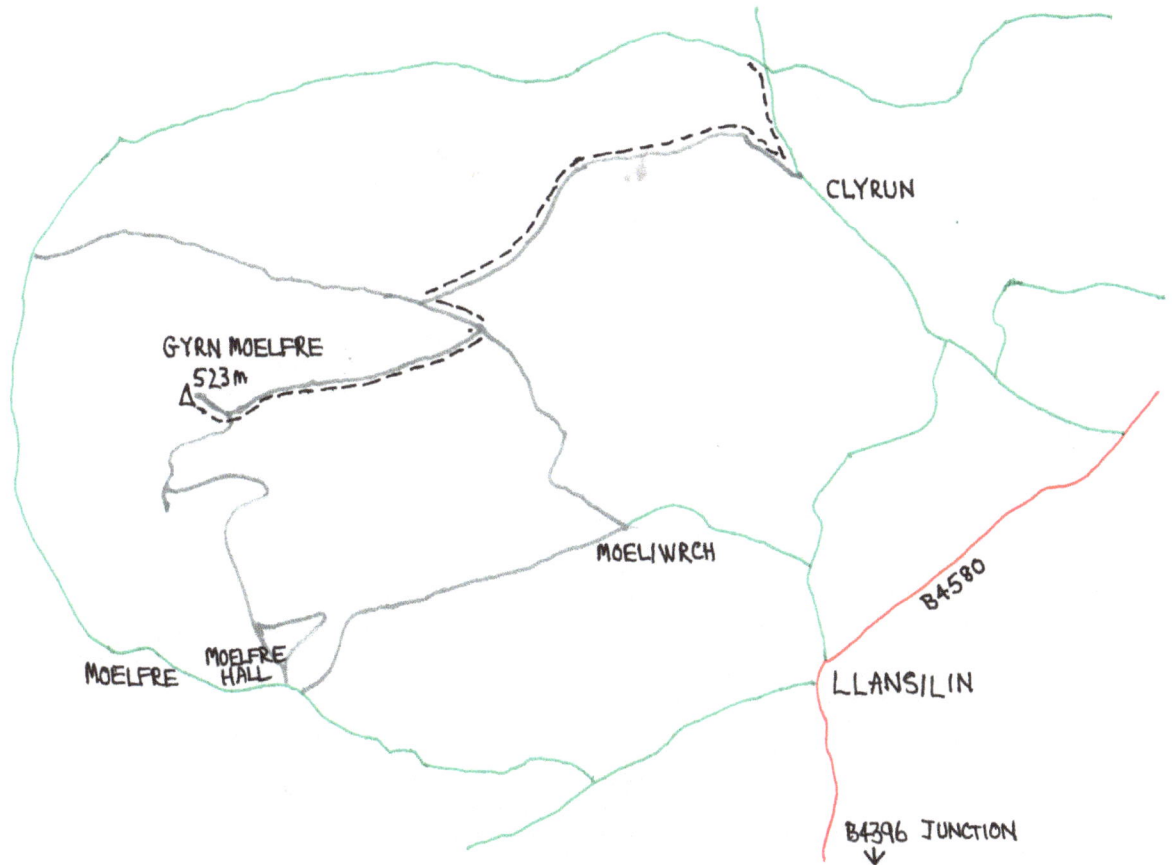

Map is about 2.5 inches to a mile with the walk shown as a dashed line.
This walk takes about three hours, including time to enjoy views, fauna and flora.

Gyrn Moelfre is a dominant mountain from Penybont on account of its height and its block of cheese shape. These days, cheese comes in rectangular blocks but in the past and that's what you dwell on when you get older, cheese was cut in the shape of Gyrn Moelfre. I well remember Mum buying a pound of Cheddar and it was cut with a wire on a wooden board and, when we got it home, it was stored in the cheese dish of the Gyrn shape that I still have. Looking at Gyrn Moelfre from Penybont, there is a steep slope on the left and a much more gradual slope on the right. They are known as the scarp slope and dip slope respectively. Anyway, what matters is not what they are called but the difficulty of the climb. If you want a short but really steep ascent, you go straight up the path from Moelfre Hall. There is a car park by the hall with a £5 honesty box. If you find steep slopes a little daunting, as I do these days, you choose the dip slope and this is the route I've marked on the map.

To save typing, I'm informing you now that Gyrn Moelfre is known locally as The Gyrn. There are other Gyrns but as this is the only one referred to in this book, let's just call it Gyrn. Gyrn is said to mean "horns". I don't know which horns exactly are referred to. The shape of the mountain does not convey that idea. Anyway, some time ago, that's the name they gave it so we'll let it be.

The Gyrn was the site used for the film *The Englishman who went up a Hill and came down a Mountain*. A number of local people were included in the film. The correct site of the story is in Glamorgan at Garth Hill but due to urban sprawl, the awful pattern so common in this little island, the more rural setting of the Gyrn was chosen. Garth Hill was just shy of 1000 feet in height so they increased it by 16 feet with earth to attain the official mountain status. Of course, The Gyrn is already a mountain but, for the film, they still went through the process of adding earth to make the film fit the story. The film is set in 1917 during the First World War but the film was made in 1995. The idea was all about boosting morale and self-esteem after the ravages of the war that had cost so many lives and caused so much destruction.

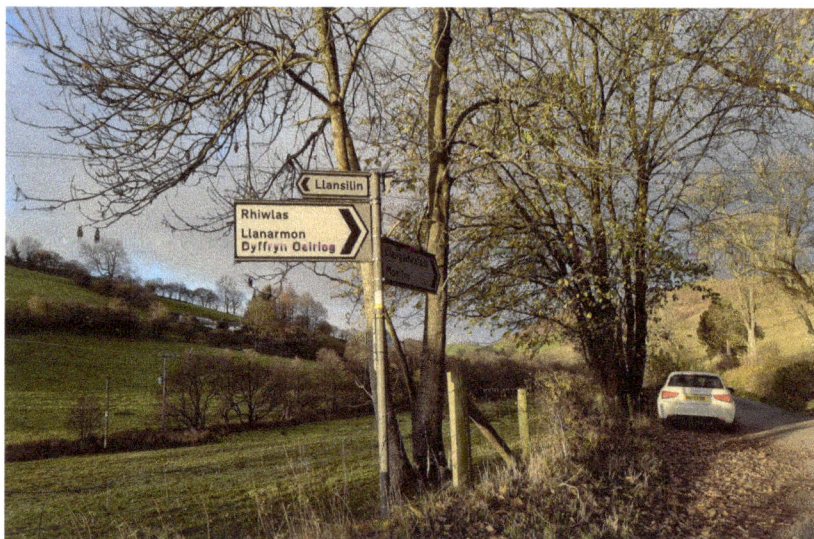

Place to park

From Penybont, you drive to Llansilin. In Llansilin, you drive through the village and take the second left. If you take the first left, you end up by Moelfre Hall, so you take the second left and end up at Clyrun. Just past Clyrun there is a left turn where you can safely stop out of the way. Don't get parking in gateways or passing places. It isn't right or fair and such behaviour can have deserved consequences. Park out of the way and everyone will be happy and, if you have to walk a bit further, it's good exercise.

From the junction, walk back up the lane towards Clyrun. You can turn immediately right once you have crossed the stream and walk over the cattle grid. Then you immediately turn left and steeply ascend the field keeping to the left side hedge. At the top of the field, there is a gate allowing you access onto the track. The field is a very steep ascent. I prefer to walk further up the lane towards Clyrun and take the next right turn. The track meets the same point you would have reached by walking up the field and it's a more gradual ascent.

The track is signed "Gyrn" and you walk up to the farm where you will be thrilled if you are into old things. Against the wall of the farm there is a cast iron corn mill. It was made by Samuel Corbett of Wellington Shropshire. This phrase is cast into the iron "The World's Best Grinding Mill". It probably was and importantly, it harks back to the time when Britain made its own stuff. The general principle now is that nearly everything you own is made in China. Why did we let this happen? This mill would originally have had a wooden hopper into which the wheat grains would have been poured. The flour would have been used on the farm and probably, the ladies from miles around would have come with their bags for flour to bake for their families.

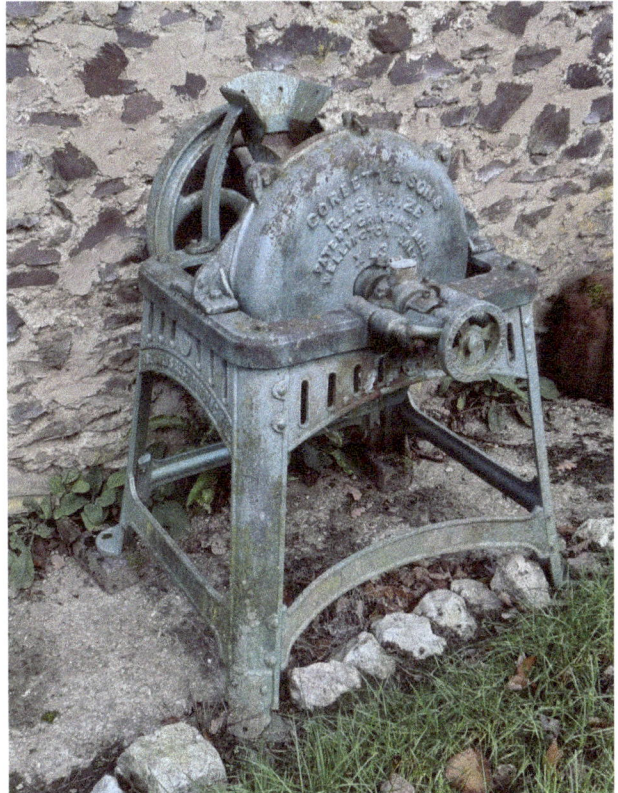

The World's Best Grinding Mill

The farm has also made a nice little feature out of the stream that comes down the hillside opposite the house. They have constructed a cascade and it's quite pretty.

Past the farm there is a gate that is heavy and ill mounted. Carefully let yourself through and shut and fasten the gate again. Continue up the track. The views open beautifully to the right and ahead you see the track ascending Gyrn. Ahead there is a boggy stretch of about 30 yards with a gate in the middle. Pick your way through as best as you can and shut the gate behind you. Continue uphill until eventually you come to an acute left hand turn. Take this turn and head uphill until you reach a gate. Through this gate you turn right and now you are on the ridge which allows wonderful views to left and right all the way to the top. You follow the ridge up the left hand side of a stone wall. There are a few stiles to climb over until eventually you arrive at the trig point at a height of 523m (1700ft in our nomenclature). Interestingly, it's still the same height above sea level despite them telling us that the sea is rising. The sea rises twice a day but it tends to go back again. King Canute tried to stop it but he was unsuccessful. He sat on his throne on the beach and commanded the tide to stay where it was. It didn't. They measure mountain heights above sea level using tide gauges and it's quite a performance. However, Gyrn is 523m high and if you look on previous OS maps, it's still the same.

This is where to make the acute turn and ascend to the Gyrn ridge

The Gyrn trig point

The view from the top is wonderful. If you look at the trig point observantly, you will notice a plaque in memory of Phylis and Winston Wilkes and describes the point as "on top of the World". Indeed it does feel like that up here. Further enquiries reveal that this couple were well known in the area. Phylis came into the village of Llansilin later in her life and was known for good works in the community. Thus the couple are remembered affectionately.

You no doubt have a snack and your trusty hip flask with you and, having fortified yourself, you make your way downhill again. At this height, it's usually cold and windy and when it's hailing, it stings a lot. It isn't a place where you want to hang about too long. You can get out of the wind in the lee of the stone wall and that's the place to rest awhile and reflect on the beauty around you before making the return walk to civilisation. Civilisation is the term loosely used to describe the social and cultural organisation in which we find ourselves on a day to day basis. In many places, civilisation hasn't advanced very far. As the Scriptures say, we have arrived at a time when there is much running to and fro and knowledge has been increased. Now we can flick a switch and the lights come on but some flick switches that are connected to advanced weaponry and wipe many people out. Some people live in luxury while others have to manage on little and some live in squalor. Some are obese while many are malnourished. Some have good healthcare while others survive as long as they don't fall ill. We use the term "civilisation" but, it has a long way to go before it fits our organisation properly.

The top of the Gyrn may be cold and windy but there is a peace and beauty that sometimes we miss in our daily lives.

South view from the Gyrn

Walk 8 – Gravel Hill

3 miles when walking from Tyn y Rhos and 6 miles return from Llangedwyn. Up-hill for the first half and downhill on the return.

Map is about 2.5 inches to a mile with the walk shown as a dashed line.
This walk takes about three hours if walking from Llangedwyn village or, one and a half hours if walking from Tyn-y-Rhos, including time to enjoy views, fauna and flora.

G ravel Hill is named on the Ordnance Survey maps. Yet the locals have not heard of this name. To them, it's Vicarage Hill. I'm using the name "Gravel Hill" because it's official but, if you ask a local the way to Gravel Hill, don't be surprised by a blank look. There is no trig point on top but, apparently the Romans had a fort up there and added about thirty foot to the top so that their beacons could be seen from distant hills. Indeed, when you get on the top, there is evidence of a fort with a bund all the way round. It was a fort earlier in the Iron Age. It is a straight forward short climb with wonderful views and, well worth the effort.

From Penybont, drive to Llangedwyn. Through the village, there is a turn on the left that take you to Bwlch y Ddar. Just after making this turn, there is a car park on the right. You can park there and walk up to the main road. Turn right and then next left. Carry on walking to the cross-roads where you will turn left. I was instructed for the climb to drive through Llangedwyn and take the Y fork on the right after the village. The lane takes you round the back of Gravel Hill. However, the road is very deep in farm laid detritus and there is no parking place. All you get from this way is an exceedingly filthy car. You can drive up to the crossroads from Llangedwyn and turn right. There is room to park your car on the wide verge on the right but, it's on the slant and, unless you don't mind off road driving, parking in the village is fine. You can always drive up there and if it seems out of your comfort zone, return to the village.

Anyway, from the crossroads, you walk towards Wern-Las. You will have to pick your way through the detritus until you come to a gate on the left and a clear view of the track spiralling up Gravel Hill.

Gravel Hill from Llangedwyn car park

Path up Gravel Hill

Go through the gate and secure it carefully behind you. Then make you way diagonally across the field and then turn left and up to another gate. Through this gate, which should also be carefully fastened, you are on a wide grassy track that takes you up to the summit. It is worth walking round the circular rampart from which, great views in all directions can be obtained. Looking north-wards across the Tanat Valley, there is first the Highland ridge and beyond that, you can see The Breiddens. To the east is the Wrekin in the distance. The Berwyn range lies to the west.

Southeast from Gravel Hill. Wrekin in rear centre, then The Breiddens, then Highland Lane Hills

Enjoy the views. Hopefully, you have brought a picnic and your hip flask to sustain, nourish and rest awhile before making the return journey. This will be the same way as you ascended. Though this climb is relatively short, especially if you have climbed from Tyn y Rhos, there are many wonderful scenes. The rampart reminds of earlier years. You are in the proximity of those whose concern was defending themselves and the territory they had conquered. To them, this was an outpost of the Roman Empire. The rampart is the perimeter of a hill fort. There is a marked pimple on one end of this hill and, that was apparently added by the Romans to increase the height of the hill by about thirty feet so that the beacon on top could signal to the next one in the Llansantfraid area. Below the Roman fort are the Iron Age remains that were excavated in about 1983 and evidence of iron smelting on the site was found with lots of interesting artefacts. Eventually, the Roman Empire was to collapse from within. You wonder how the command went out to withdraw folk from Britain to prop up the declining empire. Anyway, they vacated this stronghold and left behind their earthworks.

Westwards from Gravel Hill

We can still appreciate the same views. We can still have a picnic up here. Ours may be in a plastic box instead of an earthenware pot or a leather bag. But the principle is the same. This wonderful creation is to be appreciated as many generations have done before.

Aran Hill and mast from Gravel Hill

Walk 9 – The Green Inn

8 miles. Uphill for the first quarter, then down to the Green Inn, then level to Llangedwyn, then uphill to Highland Lane and downhill to finish.

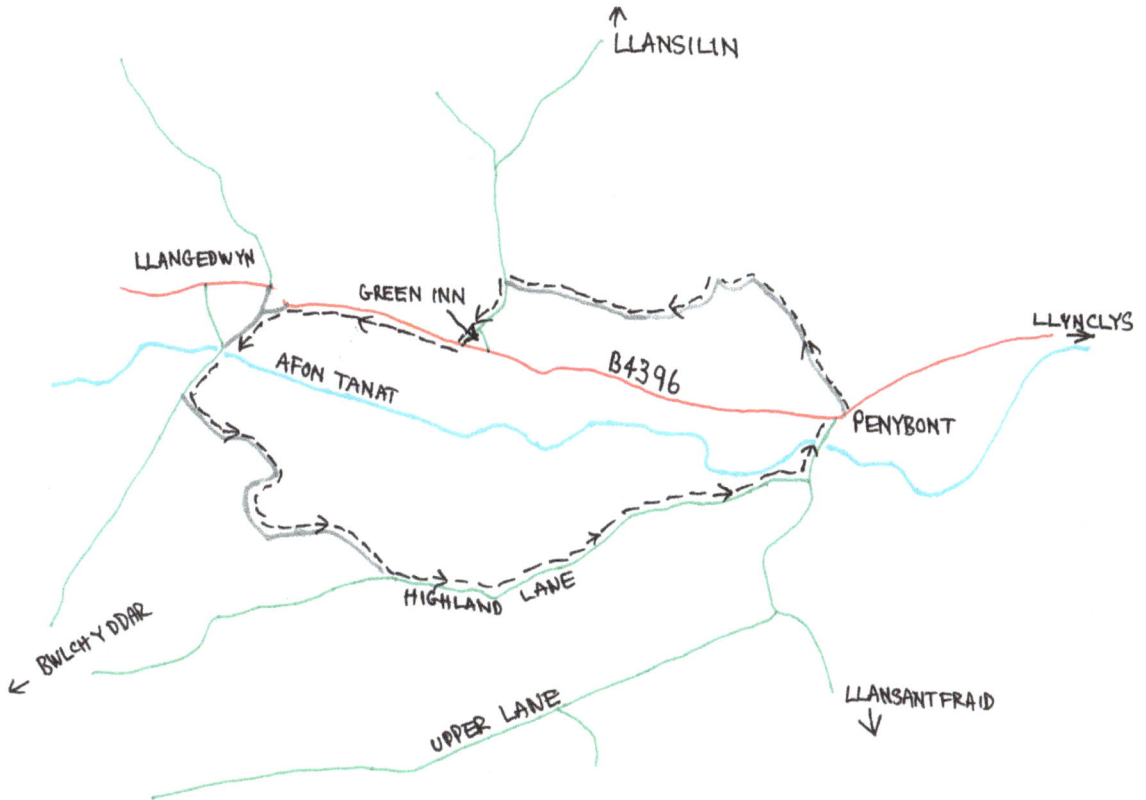

Map is about 2.5 inches to a mile with the walk shown as a dashed line.
This walk takes about four hours, including time to enjoy views, fauna and flora.

Opposite the front entrance to Penybont Inn is an iron railing constructed from different sections, gates, mesh and plate. This is the start of the walk. Climb over with care. It is chicken proof as the B4396 is not hospitable for wandering fowl. The only question would be the number of seconds they would survive. Penybont has a thirty miles per hour speed limit but, there is no physical method of slowing the traffic to that speed so, only the minority of drivers with some social skills, bother to adhere to it. Most come through at forty or thereabouts and a significant number roar through at motorway speeds. The fastest clocked speed through the village was sixty seven and when the traffic officer isn't present with the detection apparatus, the speeds are truly alarming. This is antisocial behaviour in a village inhabited by people with their children, their pets and their chickens.

Anyway, you cross the chicken and pet proof barrier and the hopeful and friendly creatures will be interested in you. Keep going along the right hand hedge. There is a small hill on your left and once you have passed it, you turn diagonally left and make your way gradually uphill across the field come to a gate. Go through the gate, closing it securely behind you. In front of you there is a copse topped hill. When you cross the next field, there is a gate at the bottom of the trees. Through the gate, you are on a track. Turn left and keep to the track about half way round the copse. Then turn partly left and climb gradually across the field to the summit.

Friendly hen, Penybont

In front of you is a line of trees that lead down to the lane from the Green Inn to Llansilin. You cross a stile and follow the trees to the lane.

Follow the lane left down to the Green Inn. This lane is quiet but bendy and having poor visibility. Keep your eyes and ears open for vehicles. Walk in front of the Green Inn, which if open, will provide some nice cool refreshment. If not, never mind, disappointment is the author of alternative strategies. You will fish your own refreshments out of your rucksack and avail yourself of the seating on the green in front of the Inn and sustain your body for the next part of the walk.

Stile and line of trees on the right to follow to Llansilin Lane

From the Green Inn you turn right and walk along the B4396 to Llangedwyn. This is relatively safe as there is a pavement along this section and the road is straight. On your right is an interesting multi-sided structure in the field. This was apparently a stable for the horses of the stately home that you can see as you approach Llangedwyn. This stately home is Llangedwyn Hall and was the seat of Sir Watkin Williams-Wynn. The estate owns a huge amount of land in the area.

When you reach Llangedwyn, the church is on your left. Cross the road and take the footpath immediately after the church. This leads downhill into a field. The footpath actually crosses this field diagonally to the far right hand corner but, if there is a crop in the field, as there sometimes is, you can skirt the field to arrive at the same place just before the river. Here there is a stile which you climb over. Opposite the stile is the site of Llangedwyn Mill which was one of several mills on the Afon Tanat.

Turn left and follow the lane for a short distance towards Bwlch y Ddar. You cross the Tanat on the bridge and follow the lane past Home Farm. Immediately after the farm, turn left up a track. Follow this track uphill. There are lovely views across the Tanat valley on the left and pine woods on the right. Continue up the track and after about half a mile, you will come to the bat sanctuary at Hendre. You will probably recognise this from Walk 3. Now you follow the track in the reverse order of Walk 3, heading upwards through lovely Larch woods and eventually you come to Highland Lane. Here you turn left and follow Highland Lane back to Penybont. Note the lovely views on the left towards the Gyrn.

Crossing the Afon Tanat in Llangedwyn

The last time I walked this route, a thunderstorm occupied the middle of it. The thing with a thunderstorm is the amount of water that can fall in a short time. Trees provide welcome shelter but after a few minutes the rain starts to come through. They say you shouldn't shelter under trees in these conditions. Trees do get struck and if you are underneath, you share the lightning on its way to the earth. I did shelter and by the time the rain came through, the worst was over. It was all very beautiful and one is always struck, hopefully not by the lightning but, by seeing the power of it. The roar of the thunder puts you in your place and makes you feel rather small and vulnerable.

The Green Inn is to the left. Central is the hill that forms most of this walk. Behind is the Gyrn.

Walk 10 – Llangedwyn East

6 miles. Level for 2 miles, then uphill to Bwich-y-ddar. Then downhill for 2 miles.

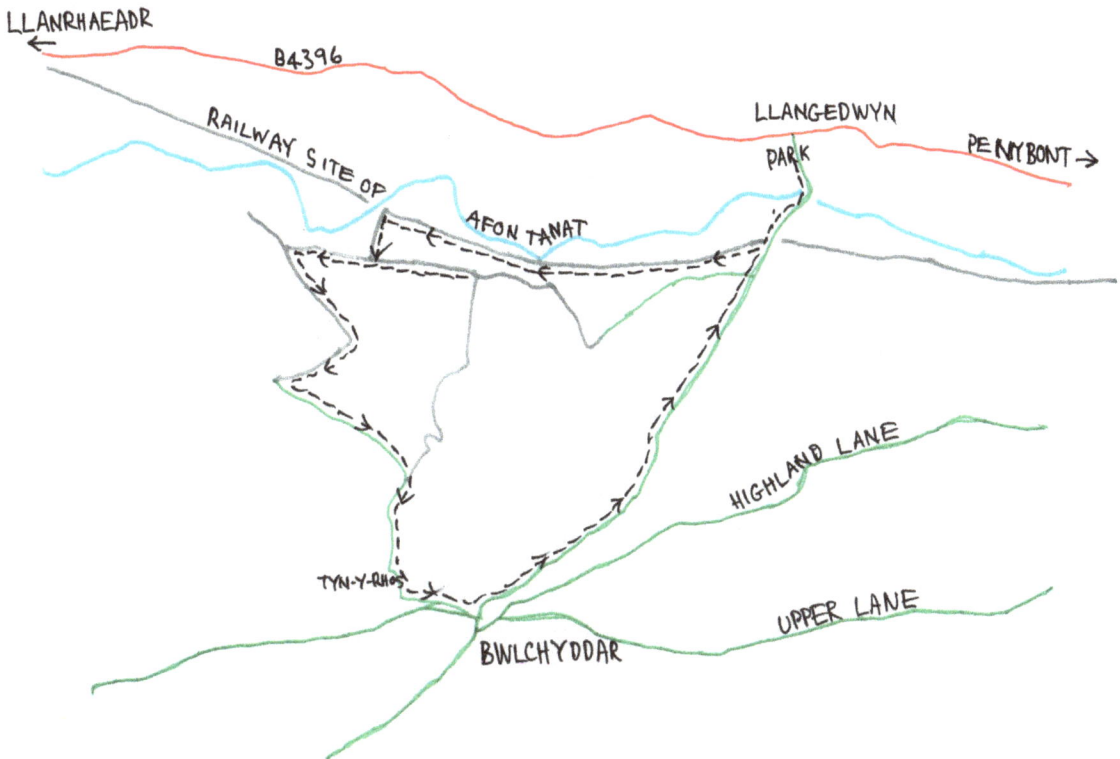

Map is about 2.5 inches to a mile with the walk shown as a dashed line.
This walk takes about three hours, including time to enjoy views, fauna and flora.

Drive from Penybont to Llangedwyn. Through the village, take the left turn just before the school. After a few yards there is a car park on the right just before the old mill, home to the Antur Tanat Cain trust. This is a truly wonderful collection of buildings that were on the site of the mill some of whose artefacts and history remain today. The main iron mill axle remains in the grounds. Also a crane used for tasks like loading pit props was used in days when Britain was self-sufficient in energy. Coal provided solid fuel and also gas. Most plastics in the past were produced from coal.

Anyway, having parked your conveyance, walk up the lane towards Bwlch-y-ddar and cross the Tanat using the bridge. Just after the bridge you will see Llangedwyn Home Farm on the left and on the right there is a gate and the dismantled railway track towards Llanrhaeadr. Close the gate behind you and proceed up the track bed for about one and a half miles. There are a few bridges to cross. Their structure has been severely dealt with by the ravages of nature over time. Some are fine to cross but some are dodgy. I tend to stick to the iron beams if you can see them.

There is mostly the opportunity to descend and walk past the bridge and ascend again to the track bed. At one point you have to go through a gate on your right and walk through nettles and up to the track again. For this reason, this walk is best tackled before May, while the nettles are still at low level.

Tanat railway has seen better days

Enjoy the views across the Tanat towards Gravel Hill and The Gyrn and, the Berwyn range further up the valley. After one and a half miles of this level walk, you come to the bridge that took the railway over the river. The bridge has gone. This is a bit sad for those who would like to see the reinstatement of a good national rail network that served all communities. This is pretty much what Britain had but, it was not liked by those who had the say and much of the network was scrapped. It would be grand to see steam engines making their way up the Tanat Valley to Llangynog but, that is a dream that will remain unfulfilled. The reinstatement of this line becomes more difficult by the year as its track bed is increasingly being built on. Having reminisced, you look at the bits of bridge remaining and because you can't go forwards, you turn left and walk upstream.

After a few yards you come to a ford. If the Tanat is low, you could walk across but you will get your feet wet and, if you fall over, you will get all of you wet. Instead, you look left and see a stile in the hedge ahead. Cross the stile and head diagonally left to a gate. This takes you onto a track. Turn right and walk up the track.

Ford across the Tanat

After a few yards you come to a gate bearing a label asking you to close the gate. Having opened the gate and gone through, that's what you do. Then, continue up the track for about one hundred yards when you come to another gate. This one doesn't have a notice asking you to close it but, having gone through, you still keep to the country code as always and close the gate.

You now enter woodland and it was rather nice because when I last did this walk, the rain was descending in a meaningful manner and the broadleaved trees provided welcome shelter. You are at a junction where you can turn left or right. Turn left and get going steeply uphill. Ahead you will see the first of several fallen trees. If you are the Shrewsbury Town Crier who stands at seven foot two inches, scooting under a fallen tree might be an issue but, if you are five foot six and a half inches, you will cope easily. Once under the first tree, you have the measure of the thing and just repeat it further on. Some of these monster trees have been cut into sections and I counted the rings. I got to one hundred and sixty and there were still many more. This brings the lesson that even trees reach their end. They live three or four times as long as us and many times more for some trees like oaks, unless someone cuts them down. Truly life is brief and its opportunities are not to be missed.

Track towards woodland – sign says "please close the gate"

Uphill track through woods

Continue uphill until you open out into a little clearing. At this point, the track bears right and through a gate and turns into a lovely grassy walk. Continue gently downhill until you come to a house. Here there is a gate on the left and through the gate, you follow the right hand hedge for about fifty yards until you come to a lane. Here, you turn left and walk gently uphill for about half a mile. You are now above the height of Gravel Hill and looking across, the circle of its hill fort may be appreciated. You come to a T junction. Turning left takes you down a track towards the Tanat. You turn right and walk past Tyn-y-rhos and onwards to Bwlch-y-ddar. There are lovely views to the village on the way.

Once you reach Bwlch-y-ddar, you turn left and follow the lane to Llangedwyn and reunite yourself with your car. Before you leave Bwlch-y-ddar, take time to enjoy the aesthetic beauty of the old direction sign on the green in the village centre. Also take a look at the lovely collection of old buildings. The walk down the lane to Llangedwyn is easy as it's downhill all the way. It's also mostly straight and that adds to the safety because you can see the traffic and the traffic can see you. It is a fairly quiet lane but you should keep your eyes and ears open to vehicles.

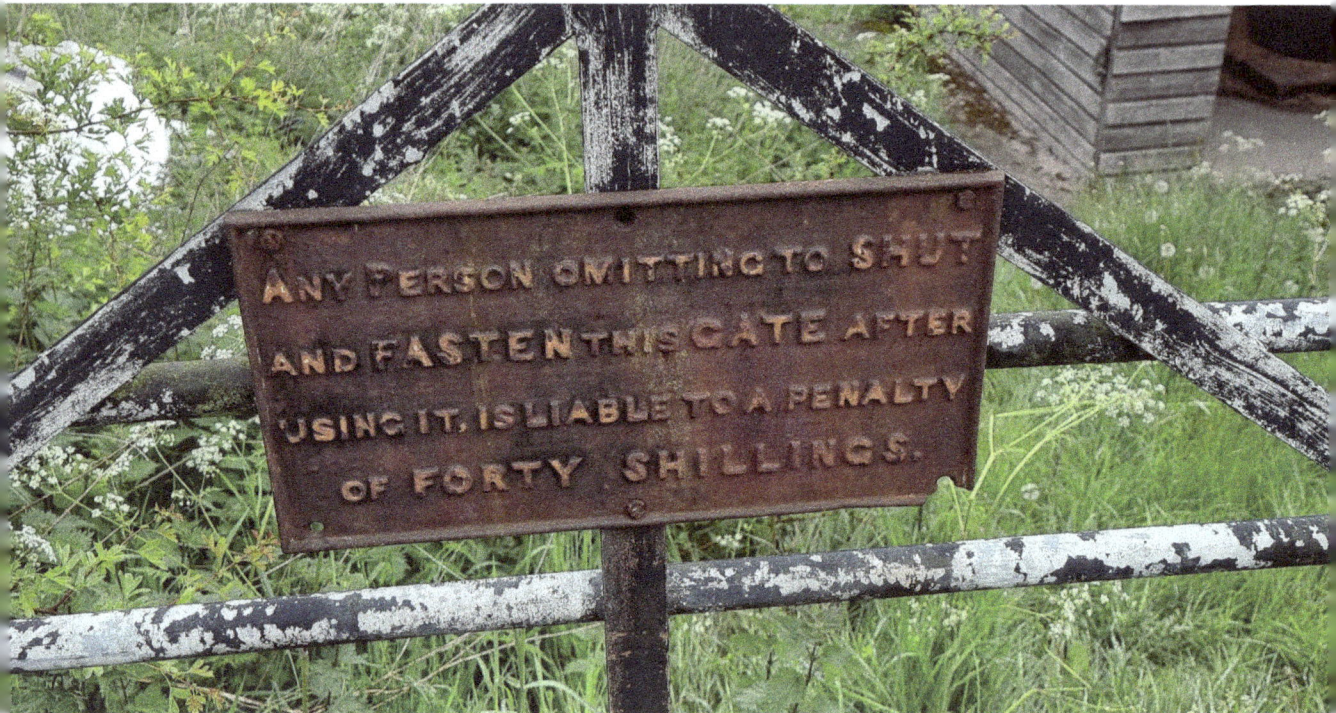

Forty shillings was a lot of money then! This sign is on a gate in Bwlch y Ddar.

The Gyrn from Bwlch y Ddar

Walk 11 – Aran Hill

2 miles. Uphill to summit and downhill on the return. Level round Llyn y Briw.

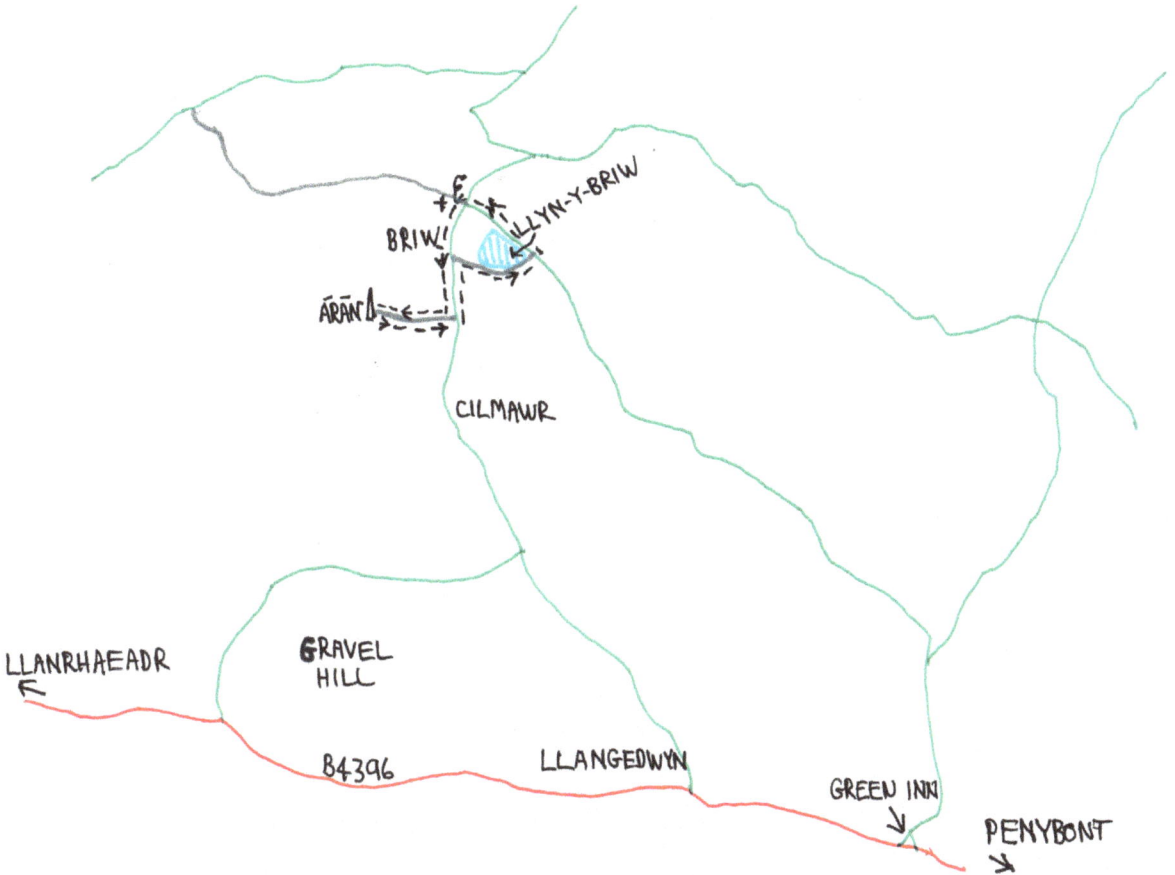

Map is about 2.5 inches to a mile with the walk shown as a dashed line.
This walk takes about two hours, including time to enjoy views, fauna and flora.

Aran Hill lies between Gravel Hill and the Gyrn, north of Llangedwyn. It is a short walk but very steep and is well worth achieving from the point of its height and views. It is surmounted by a communication mast that I'm told is EE property. EE literally stands for "Everything Everywhere". Unfortunately the meaning is not quite true here. Electromagnetic radiation, of which radio waves are part of the spectrum, tend to travel in straight lines. Wales is a land of hills and valleys and, unless you have your mast on the top of the highest hill which everyone can see, you will have dead places. If they put a filthy great mast on top of the Gyrn, it would probably be a lot more effective than the one on Aran. It would however, probably be regarded as undesirable on account of its visual impact. In theory, it is possible to make a mast invisible but, the technology has not become available yet. The invention derives from our perception of colour. Things don't actually have colour. They absorb light energy and emit light back of a particular wavelength which we perceive as the object's colour. However, you could in theory have a paint that absorbs all light frequencies and this would render the object invisible. The applications are many and varied and such paint will sell very well when it comes out. Imagine riding an invisible bike or walking on invisible stilts. It really appeals to the imagination. Your invisible EE mast would please the aesthetic requirements of the public but would be dangerous for aircraft and migrating birds. Therefore such a structure will not be installed any time soon. Besides, the paint is not yet available. When it does come out, there will be a lot of lost property and a lot of bumped heads and stubbed toes but, it will be great fun.

We digress. To walk up Aran Hill, you have a long walk from the car park in Llangedwyn. I park in Briw by the derelict phone box opposite the chapel. Here you aren't in anybody's way but, there is only room for one vehicle. There are few places to park round here.

From the phone box, or rather, what's left of it, because it has been vandalised, you walk a few yards back to the crossroads. Then walk back towards Llangedwyn for about half a mile. On the right there is a gate with a sign saying "Site Number 141010". Through this gate, you are on a steep track up to the mast. After about one hundred yards you come to a cattle grid. Make your way carefully over it and continue onwards to the summit. Stop every now and then to survey the increasingly good view to the Gyrn and Llyn-y-Briw and other features in the distance. You will have to stop frequently anyway to catch your breath unless you are very fit.

On arriving at the mast, stop and enjoy the wonderful scenery.

Aran Hill

The Gyrn and Aran Mast

The Gyrn and Llyn-y-Briw

To the right of the mast enclosure there is a stile and over the stile, you can walk on to the summit of Aran Hill and then you have the additional wonderful view across west to The Berwyns. South is Gravel Hill and the Tanat Valley beyond. You are above Gravel Hill and can look down on its hill fort that had strategic importance in Roman times and the Iron Age before then.

Having supped on the view and improved your mind with the beautiful scenery, retrace your steps down to the lane. Ensure the gate is securely fastened. Half way back to Briw is a stile on the right. Over the stile, you can follow the footpath along the hedge to Llyn-y-Briw and you can walk round the lake to the lane between Briw and the Green Inn to Llansilin road. There are lovely views across the lake to Aran summit. Take care round the lake. You have to cross an inlet stream and cope with a lot of foliage. Follow the path round to the lane. Turn left and proceed to the crossroads, over which is the phone box from which you started.

Gravel Hill and Tanat Valley

The Berwyns

Llyn-y-Briw

East with The Wrekin in the distance from Aran Hill

Walk 12 – Sycharth

4 miles. Mostly fairly level.

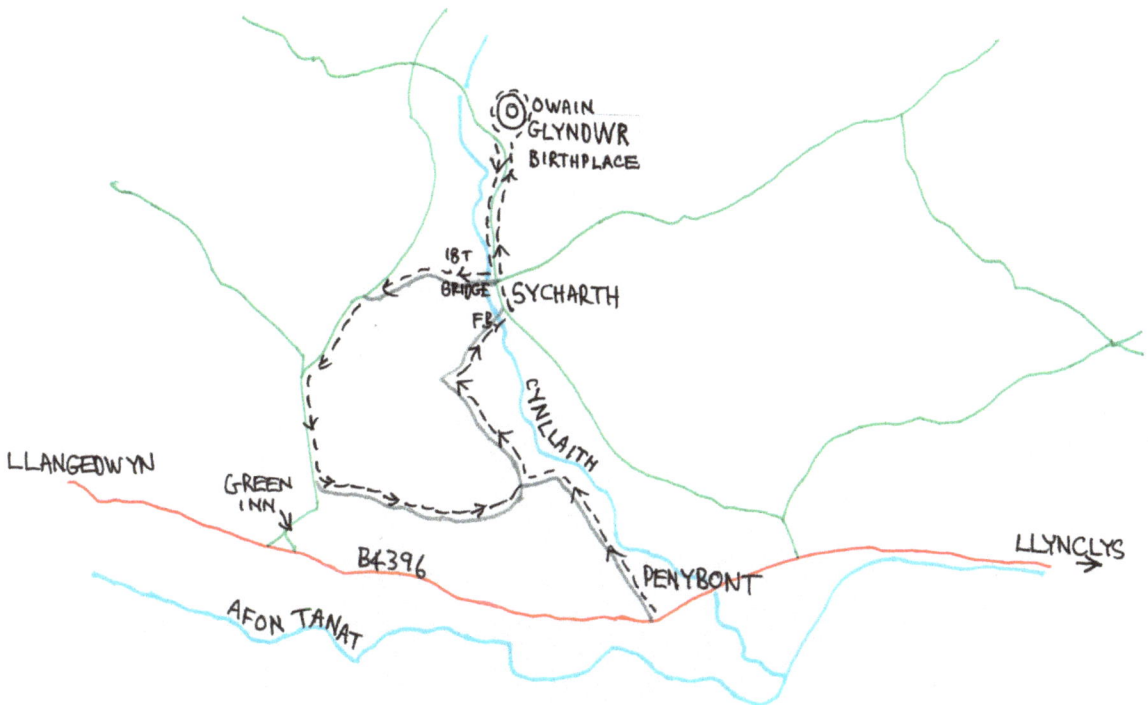

Map is about 2.5 inches to a mile with the walk shown as a dashed line.
This walk takes about two hours, including time to enjoy views, fauna and flora.

From Penybont, proceed as for Walk 9, the Green Inn, crossing over the B4396 and accessing the footpath over a sort of iron structure made up of various components at the right hand side of the old Country Store. There is a small hill on your left. Pass that on the right, keeping to the hedge. Once past this hill, proceed diagonally across the field towards a small copse with a gate at the right hand side. Through this gate, proceed upwards until you come to another gate. Proceed upwards again until you come to woodland. Here you turn right. The view back towards Penybont is lovely, as is the view ahead towards the Gyrn.

The Gyrn

Continue onwards and gradually downhill towards a farm. Here you will find a footbridge over the Cynllaith which is a considerable stream that joins the Tanat at Penybont. Over the footbridge, you turn left on the lane to Sycharth. There is a house on the right hand side called Sycharth, but you carry on. The Gyrn is ahead but don't worry about that. It is a comfort to know that you are walking in the right direction, which is north. After half a mile, you come to a Y junction and you take the right hand lane. This leads up to a little car park, suitable perhaps for a couple of cars.

The Y junction had a sign but, this is now part of the hedge and so completely embedded in it that you cannot see it.

Footbridge over the Cynllaith

I have included a photograph of the junction so that you will know when you have arrived.

The Y junction to Owain Glydwr's place. The sign is IN the hedge on the junction

Walk up to the car park. The lane continues but you don't. On the left there is a fancy stile with steps up on the car park side but, one of the treads is missing on Owain Glyndwr's side. Be careful to descend without injury. Ahead you will see the mound on which Owain Glyndwr's stronghold was built. It was a wooden structure that the English burned out. You see, British history is one of war and savagery to rival anywhere on earth. It stems from one of the basest human instincts which is the desire to be in charge and control everybody. Owain wanted independence from England and fought for it quite successfully. He was helped by the French and there's another age old source of friction. We are supposed to learn from history but, we rarely do. So the conflicts of the past live on today. The desire for peace and harmony, kindness and love between all people comes second place to wanting to control them. The trouble is that those aspiring to be in charge have the wrong aptitude for it. They are the aggressive types who are willing to embark on a course of slaughter to achieve more land, a higher position and more power. Those able and willing to do proper jobs and support others don't get to be in charge, although they would be fair and just if they were put in that position. Anyway, Owain's bid for independence eventually faltered in face of the much larger armies from England. His stronghold was burned and he resorted to guerrilla type activities later on. He was never captured or betrayed to the English and eventually died at about fifty-six years of age.

The stile to Owain Glyndwr's place

Owain Glyndwr's place

All that remains of his life at Sycharth is the grassy mound in front of you. Walk all round it and enjoy the views and think of those characters of long ago and their little idyll here that came to such a sad end. On top of the mound was a flag, set in a square stone but someone has broken it off and all that now remains is the square stone.

Returning to Penbont, you walk back down the lane until you reach a lane on the right with a bridge over the Cynllaith. The bridge is marked as "Weak" and has a weight limit of 18 tons. I don't know when it was last tested for its load carrying ability. Judging by the state of the roads round here, these things don't get attended to very often. However, it will easily take your weight, even if you have a liking for pastry. Cross over the bridge and enjoy looking at the river as you do so. It's quite pretty.

Ahead you will see a narrow lane climbing upwards. It is rather overgrown and when it's wet, it is a soaking long grass hike that bears all the hall marks of a little used trail. It climbs up to join the road between the Green Inn and Llansilin. When you reach the road you turn left. This road isn't too busy but, there is a need to be vigilant and listen out for vehicles.

Bridge for the return journey

The road continues on the level until it eventually descends in a bendy way to the Green Inn. Before then, there is a gate on the left. Through the gate you follow a line of trees uphill and eventually, you come to a stile. After the stile, you curve to the left until you join the outward route. Here you go through the gates and follow the route down to Penybont.

Make sure as always to close gates securely as the fields are occupied by sheep and cows and it is vital that you look after their security.

Walk 13 – America

4 miles. Hilly but predominantly uphill for the first half and downhill on the return.

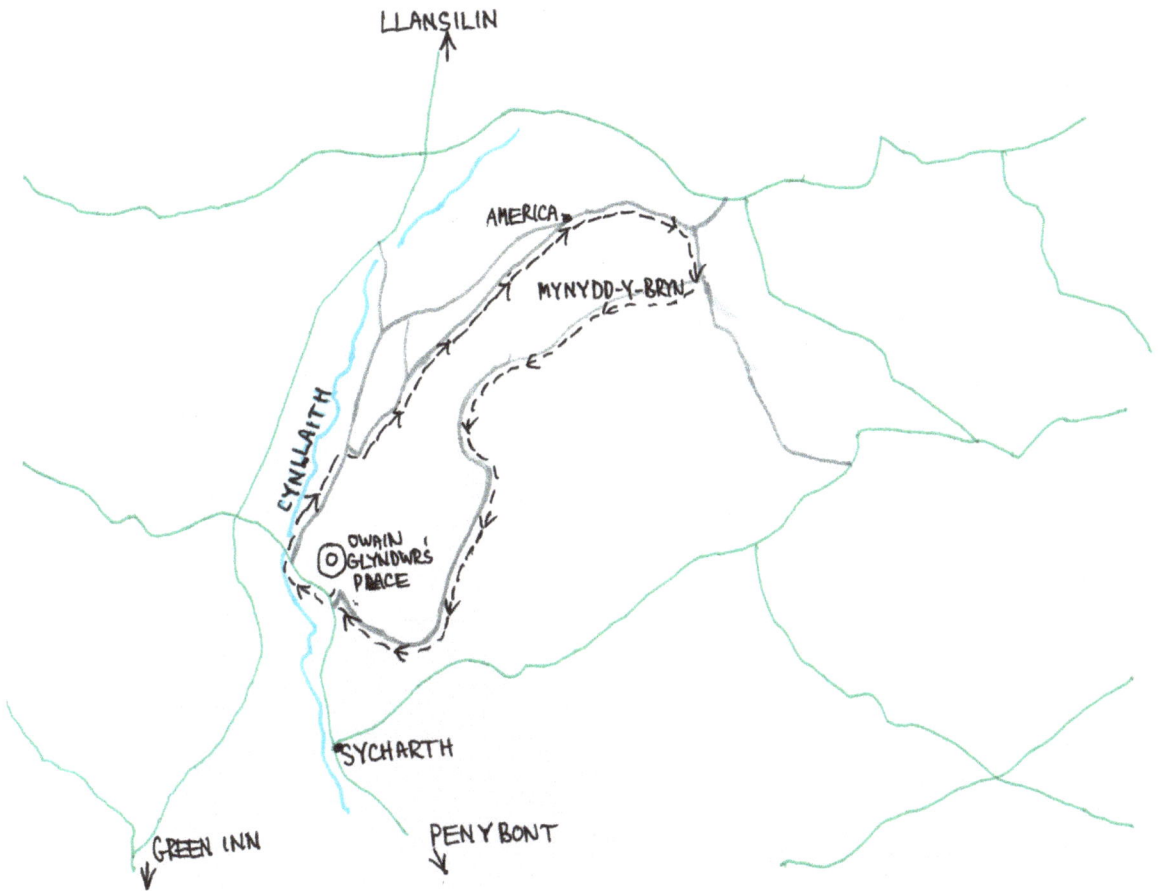

Map is about 2.5 inches to a mile with the walk shown as a dashed line.
This walk takes about two and a half hours, including time to enjoy views, fauna and flora.

If you ask someone round Penybont where the path to America is, you are thought of as having mind problems. When you are my age, it doesn't really attract abuse because they think, oh it's only him, he can't help it. The thing is that most people don't explore their surroundings. They will tell you where they work and shop, where the nearest pubs are and probably where the surgery is but, other geographical matters are hazy. Most locals haven't heard that America is near Penybont. They only know of America as a place way out west across a lot of water. America is marked on the Ordnance Survey map and is a cottage that was built by a John Williams in 1823. It was originally three cottages and was lived in as recently as 2006. If it was for sale, which it isn't, the estate agents would say that it would benefit from some sympathetic modernisation, a phrase meaning that it needs rebuilding from the inside. It has an enviable position, remote enough to escape immediate plans for turning into a city. It is far enough away from busy roads to escape traffic noise and vibration. The only disturbance likely would be from farming and livestock. You would benefit from a four wheel drive vehicle as the access is via a long track. Most people seem to aspire to this sort of conveyance today. Wealthy folk have models made by Porsche, BMW or Jaguar Land Rover whereas the ordinary folk go for Dusters, Toe Rags and Cash Cows. For a breed of motor vehicle they can generally be relied on to get in the way, be driven rather badly in a dominant manner. I used to wonder what the attraction was until I heard a group of doctors discussing their own versions of four wheel drives. One whose model was the size of a small house described with pride the way he could barge through the traffic with it and command right of passage. However, if you live in a cottage up a long muddy track, such a vehicle becomes a need rather than a status symbol.

America

You can do this walk as an extension of Walk 12 or, as a separate one as I do. It is a hilly walk and one where way finding is difficult on account of footpath damage and way marker absence. Supposing that you are doing this walk as a stand-alone exercise rather including in Walk 12, you can park in Owain Glyndwr's car park at Sycharth. Look back at Walk 12 instructions as the entrance to this car park is obscure. Having parked, make your way down to the road and turn right, heading towards Llansilin and the Gyrn mountain. After about one hundred yards, there is a galvanised footpath gate on the right. Ahead is the road bridge over the Cynllaith so, if you get to the bridge, you've gone too far. There were some folk strolling down the lane towards me and I asked if the footpath led to America. I think they felt sorry for me but seemed to regard me as harmless. The footpath leads round to the left and is very lumpy. It ends up in a field with no way markers and I wasted quite some time crossing the field, much to the interest of the young cows. I can save you this ramble by telling you to keep to the left hand hedge until you find another galvanised footpath gate. This leads into a bed of nettles which is rather unpleasant but only lasts for about fifteen yards. Soon afterwards you come to a gate that leads into a large field that was occupied by eighteen inch high grass that appeared to be growing for silage. Looking diagonally across the field towards the right, I saw a gate and made for that. It was hard work. Through the gate you are on a track. Turn left and continue gradually uphill.

After a while, you come to a gate bearing a sign telling you to proceed on foot only. Perhaps the wag who posted the sign thought you may have arrived at the point in a bus or horse and cart or something. At least the gate has a hook fastening and is so up to date compared with the normal binder twine arrangements.

The Gyrn and silage field

The gate, the mud and the unwell walked path

A little further on you falter because the track seems to run out in overgrown gardens. Again I wasted time trying to find where I was supposed to go. The answer seems to be to keep left of the properties and make your way round them. When you have negotiated this pickle successfully, you come to a sort of car park for one or more of the properties and the track onwards leads gradually downhill. To the left is a beautiful view of the Gyrn. Follow the track downhill to a Y junction. Take the right hand fork and climb uphill. To the left is a chicken shed of immense proportions and a very high fence separating you from it. A few chickens, who no doubt have found their way out of this establishment, will be interested in you. Continue on this indistinct track, gaining height all the way until you come to a gate. It is in the middle of a sea of mud but comfortingly, it does bear a footpath sign. There is no instruction to shut the gate and you won't be able to anyway because although you could lift the gate, the bolt is several inches shy of the post. Just do the best you can without shipping too much mud. There are a number of nettle beds to negotiate along the path but, as long as you do the walk before June, you should manage without a scythe. Once through the gate you continue uphill until you reach America.

At America, you should pause to absorb its subtle charms and grand position, looking down on Llansilin and across to the lovely mountains. Here the track is good. After a few hundred yards there is a gate on the right and a footpath sign leading uphill across a field. Through the gate continue as best as you can until you come to a junction. Turn right here and walk up to the top of the mountain.

Junction where you turn right

Mynydd-y-Bryn literally means mountain hill and was perhaps named by someone who wasn't sure whether it was a mountain or a hill and wanted to play it safe by giving both characteristics. Another alternative is that they were convinced it was a mountain and Bryn was the owner. With the aid of the Ordnance Survey map we can clear up the technical query by noting that this elevation is 330m or 1072ft and is therefore officially of mountain status, assuming that the qualifying height is 1000ft. There are mighty fine views from the top. To the east, you can see the Wrekin. The Breiddens lie to the southeast. To the north is Llansilin and the Gyrn behind it. The Berwyn range lies to the west.

Mynydd-y-Bryn ridge and The Berwyns

Rock in the field

Walk along the ridge. The footpath is ill defined. As you reach lower ground there is dense woodland that is private and you should keep to the left of this. After a while you find yourself in a field with a big rock incongruously in the middle of it. This will tell you that you are on the right track.

The woodland is fenced and gates into it are all marked private. Keep the woodland on the right and eventually you will see a gate ahead leading into Owain Glyndwr's car park. Though not long, this walk is far from easy and I guess, is seldom walked. It is however, full of interest from the reason why a block of cottages here would be called "America" to the beautiful views from the higher points of the walk.

Descending to Owain Glyndwr's car park. My car is the white speck in the centre.

Some parts of the walk are quite remote and the crows circling above my head created a slight unease as to whether they had diagnosed an impending meal for themselves. I did make it back to the car and still retain the enjoyable scenery in mind.

Footpath up Mynydd y Bryn

Walk 14 – Moelydd

4 miles. Uphill first half. Downhill return.

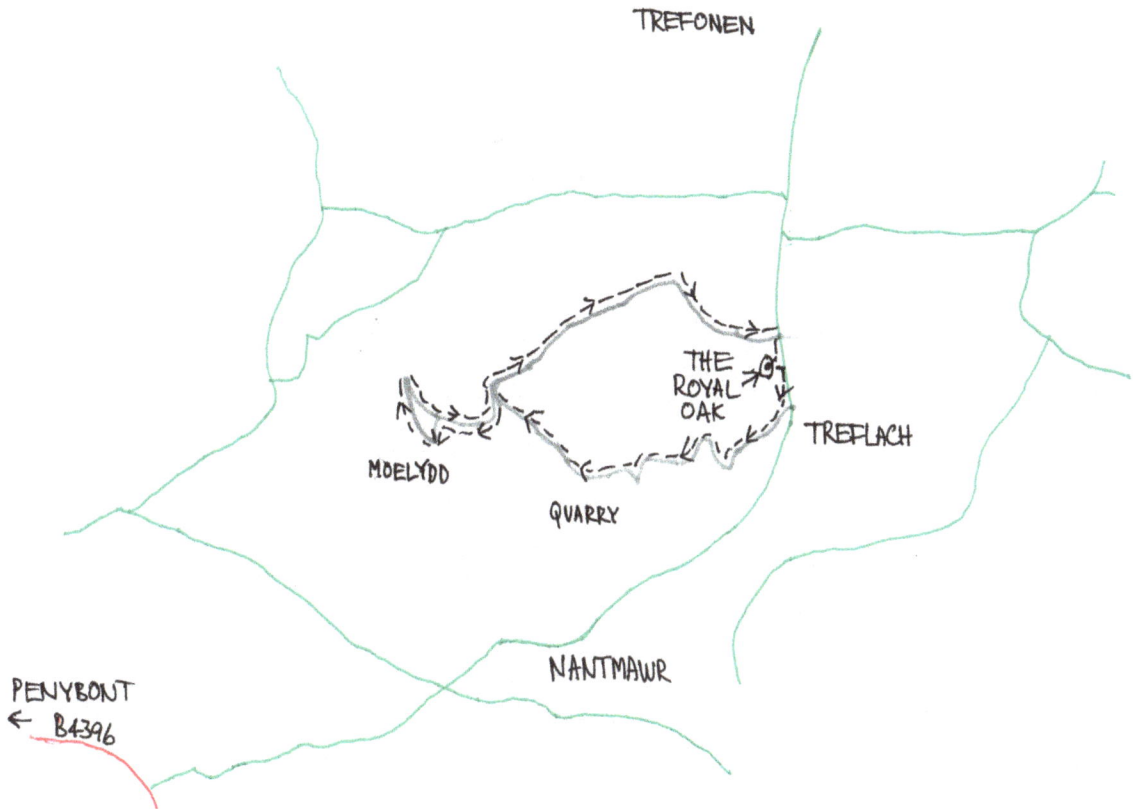

Map is about 2.5 inches to a mile with the walk shown as a dashed line.
This walk takes about two hours, including time to enjoy views, fauna and flora.

It would be improper not to include a walk with some of Offa's Dyke. Penybont is on the Welsh / English border. Twelve hundred years ago, King Offa of England, thought it would be a good idea to dig a ditch the full length of the border which was some 82 miles. The dyke path is about 173 miles which is twice the length of the original dyke. Offa's purpose was to fortify the border against Welsh incursion. His warrior activities didn't do him a lot of good and he died while it was being commissioned in a skirmish against the Welsh. England was not overpopulated then and there were only about nine million people. The idea of controlling the whole border in this manner seems a bit silly. However, that's what he tried. This is the trouble with management and politicians. They live in a world of big ideas that are silly and not thought through properly. They are usually examples of control freakism and are labour intensive and bother everyone. Why people can't live in peaceful cooperation is a mystery. The minds of the most inappropriate people concentrate on being in charge and controlling everyone. It is a fact that the law actually prohibits a Welshman from entering Chester after sundown until sunrise and it is still supposedly permissible to shoot him with a crossbow within the city walls between those times. We think of those in authority in England now as being unhinged, and as a general rule, this is sadly true. Yet history shows that little changes.

However, the dyke has now become a long distance footpath and is a delight to follow. The footpath does not often keep to the dyke and the organisers have instead chosen to seek out all the high ground from which views can be enjoyed. The result is an amazing 173 mile long distance trail. The walk over Moelydd only follows the trail for a short distance to the summit of the hill. The symbol for the Offa's Dyke path is an acorn and when you see the white acorn on posts, you know you are on Offa's Dyke path. Why choose an acorn? Well, I don't know but there were a lot more oak trees when Offa was around. Since then they've steadily cleared the ancient woodlands and built roads and housing estates where they were. The acorn signs were originally carved from wood, sometimes oak. Then they went through a phase of using metal but, you've probably guessed; now they are plastic. The symbol that would perhaps best represent English activity would be a teapot but, for whatever reason, the choice was made of an acorn and we have to leave it there.

Fields Lane

Moelydd is said to mean a bare or treeless hill. There are trees but it is certainly clear enough to gain 360 degrees of views from the summit. Moelydd is a hill of 285m (935ft). A good starting and finishing point for this walk is The Royal Oak in Treflach which is on the main road through. You get there from Penybont by travelling down the B4396 towards Llynclys for two miles until you come to a left turn signed to Treflach and Trefonen. You go through Nantmawr first and here is a word of caution. The road into Nantmawr is blind and there is usually some nutty parking on the left hand side which necessitates you pulling onto the wrong side of the blind bend to continue. This needs tackling with care as a lot of drivers fly round in the hope that nothing will be coming. You progress through Nantmawr and climb uphill until you enter Treflach. The Royal Oak is on the left hand side. Always show the courtesy of asking before parking there and, be good enough to give some custom. This establishment offers an excellent range of drinks and a very nice menu. I thoroughly recommend it.

Leaving the pub car park, you turn right and after a few yards, come to Fields Lane – see above. After a short distance you come to a Y junction. Take the left hand lane. After another short distance you come to a property drive and on the right hand side you see a narrow path. That is your route. After a while you see an abandoned caravan in a smashed state. I only mention this so you know you are on the right route. By the time you do the walk, it may have been moved but, it's been there for years so I doubt it. After this you see a stile on the right and you can go over that and across the field to another stile diagonally opposite. I normally carry on round the field on the track that brings you to the same point. Just afterwards there is a stile on the left and an uphill path through trees. You come to a T junction. Turn left up the track. At the top, bear right and across a field with a company premises on your right hand side.

At the end of the field there is a "kissing gate" which admits two people if they are in a close embrace. Alternatively, you can admit one person and hold the gate back until they have submitted to your charms. I've not had this experience and have learned instead to absorb the scenery around me which is rather pleasant. Whatever your romantic options, this could be the place to exercise them.

The kissing gate signs show walks in all sorts of directions. You descend steps to a crossroads and continue opposite up the track which brings you to Nantmawr Quarry. This is a deep working and there are an absurd number of signs telling you rather tersely to keep out. Walking round the rim gives you some fantastic views towards the Breiddens and Long Mountain.

Kissing gate

Nantmawr Quarry view

As you go past the quarry, turn half right and through a gate with a funny slanted bolt fastening.

The gate with the funny fastening bolt

Look out for this path as it is a narrow junction off the main track round the quarry. Follow this path through a field with some strange humps in as if it is a skateboard experimental course. You come out by a very large heap of manure and an electric fence, neither of which want touching. You meet a wide track on a hairpin bend. Turn left and uphill. You are now on Offa's Dyke path. Follow this upwards to a gate and stile. The sign on the gate is "Ty Uchaf". Over the stile, walk uphill to the summit of Moelydd. There is a toposcope on the summit showing you directions to other high points.

Walk along Moelydd ridge to gain full benefit from the views at the south end of the ridge towards Welshpool. Retrace your steps down to the hairpin bend where you met it before. Continue down the track round two sides of a field until you come to a gate and stile. You will be stunned at the gate for it leads to a high quality tarmac drive for a mile. It was the subject of controversy back in 2019 as this drive was resurfaced wonderfully when most of the local roads were deteriorating rows of potholes. The controversy centred round the persons supplied by this lane. The whole episode was ventilated in the press at the time. Of course, George Orwell passed the remark in *Animal Farm* that all animals are equal but some are more equal than others. Thus it has always been. I recall a big cheese who had all sorts of things done and of course, it was nothing to do with his position; it was just how it worked out! We are supposed to swallow these things.

Moelydd toposcope

The nice lane

Anyway, you proceed along the nice surface as far as the sign post in the photograph. Here you turn right and make your way through nettle and thistle beds to the top of the rise in front of you. Diagonally left and downhill, you will see a gate in the far hedge. Make for this and go directly across the next field as well. When you go through the far gate you are on a track.

Turn left and continue to a house on the left and well hidden stile on the right just after the house. The house at the time of writing has had cracks in the wall repaired. When you come along, the cracks may be painted but for a long time, it is as said and this acts as a landmark for you to find the stile. The stile is marked with a blue disc referring to a WW1 trail. Over the stile, you are in a field with a lot of brown gloopy patches together with the creatures that have placed them there. Proceed through two fields keeping to the right hand hedge. In the second field there is another stile in the right hand hedge. This also bears a blue WW1 disc. Over the stile, you cross the next field behind some huge barns. Turning diagonally left after the barns, you come to a stile and gate by a bungalow. This admits you to a lane across which there is another stile. Over this you are in the last field. Cross this and you are on the Treflach to Trefonen road.

The well hidden stile at the left hand side of the gate

Turn right and after a few yards, you are back at the Royal Oak. Hopefully, you will have timed the conclusion of your walk to coincide with this lovely establishment being open so that you can oil your mechanism with a beverage.

Boots off Reflection

I hope that you have enjoyed exploring Penybont and her surroundings. God has given us a beautiful world but even after travelling far, the Tanat valley is a joy and home for me. There are other walks that could have been included but, this little collection gives the flavour of the area and her views.

All the seasons have their pros and cons. Winter gives the furthest views without the leaves to get in the way, but it's usually cold and the sensible creatures with wings have gone south. Spring is my favourite time when all the greens are fresh and bright and everything is bursting with vitality. The hedges are still low enough to get good views. The days are long and flowers glow and birds sing through the day before the stresses of parenthood occupy their full attention. Summer is also lovely but the clarity of the air is less and the hedges are high and soon the longest day is past. Autumn is folding up time. It is a time of browns and though beautiful, is a time of preparation for the long cold season. Dead leaves crunch underfoot as they fall from the hibernating trees. Squirrels gather nuts and bury them and then forget the hiding place. It's a time for gathering the fruits of the earth and many free offerings are available on our walks from mushrooms to nuts. Sloes are usually abundant and gathering them is a fiddly and prickly job but, the gin that you will make is a wonderful warming experience for the cold months. *Food for Free* by Richard Mabey is an excellent guide to what can be gathered and eaten from your walks. Much of this information is passed down through the generations but, a long time ago, people must have tried things out for the first time. The results must have been interesting and sometimes, disconcerting.

Walks in the Tanat valley are mostly stress free and stress reducing even and therefore of medical and mental benefit. News comes in daily of gridlock on the main roads and motorways and huge delays at airports. The last two years have seen travel plans put on hold unless you had exceptional circumstances or were part of the government or their advisors. Now the lid has been lifted off the travel opportunities, the industry isn't prepared for it. I know what I'd choose out of a four hour walk in the countryside or a four hour queue in an airport terminal.

Tanat valley walks are as fulfilling and memorable as any long distance travel experience. You will recount the day you fell face first into a bed of nettles, the day the sun came out and you have a stunning photograph to prove it and the day you found a giant puffball and enjoyed the grilled steaks when you got it home.

Happy wandering

Also by Peter Keen

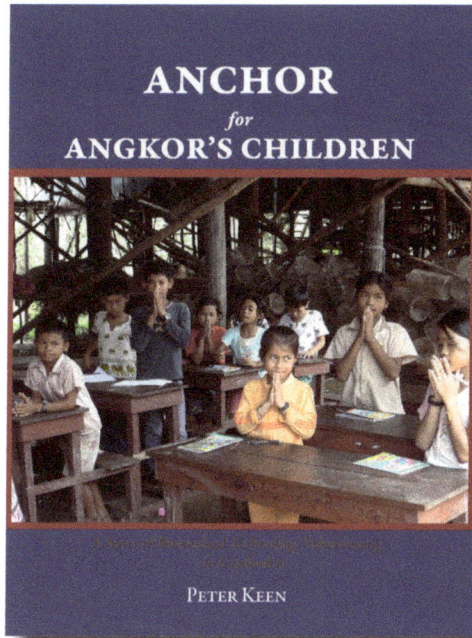

In this sincere, 'bolts and all' account, Peter Keen, a technical support volunteer in Cambodia, draws attention to the work of the *Angkor Hospital for Children*. It is a record of real people in live situations. The *Angkor Hospital for Children* is an organisation that has changed and continues to change the lives of many children in Cambodia.

There is no safety net or social security in Cambodia. Families and friends are all important when times are tough.

Peter Keen's photographs and descriptions give an insight into the work already achieved, and reveal a nation whose people shine out as examples of love and care.

This book has been produced with the sole aim of raising sufficient funds to purchase test equipment for the service and repair of the medical equipment at *Angkor Hospital for Children* and to assist in further training of Biomedical Engineers at the hospital.